GREAT ANIMALS
OF THE MOVIES

Other books by the author:

GREAT MONSTERS OF THE MOVIES
THE BOOK OF PROPHECY
VISIONS OF TOMORROW
FUNNY MEN OF THE MOVIES
GREAT MOVIE SPECTACULARS
TOUGH GUYS AND GALS OF THE MOVIES
GREAT KIDS OF THE MOVIES

EDWARD EDELSON

GREAT ANIMALS of the MOVIES

Doubleday & Company, Inc.
Garden City, New York

Library of Congress Cataloging in Publication Data

Edelson, Edward, 1932–
Great animals of the movies.

Includes index.
SUMMARY: Discusses the role of animals in films and
profiles some of the more famous stars of the screen such
as Lassie, Francis the talking mule, Mr. Ed, and Cheetah.
1. Animals in moving-pictures—Juvenile literature.
2. Animal films—History and criticism—Juvenile literature.
[1. Animals in motion pictures. 2. Animal films
—History and criticism] I. Title.
PN1995.9.A5E3   791.43'0909'36
ISBN: 0-385-14728-7 Trade
0-385-14729-5 Prebound
Library of Congress Catalog Card Number 79–8015

9 8 7 6 5 4 3 2

Contents

GREAT ANIMALS
OF THE MOVIES

Chapter One

IN THE BEGINNING

Actors hate animals.

Audiences love animals.

Those two facts are directly related. Actors don't like animals because almost any animal can steal a scene from even the best actors simply by making an appearance. Just bring a puppy or a horse or an elephant onto a stage and all the human stars immediately become bit players. If the animal can do a trick or two, the human actors might as well go home.

So from the earliest times until today, from the simplest forms of entertainment to the most sophisticated, animals have been an essential part of what we now call show business. One whole branch of show business, the circus, is built on animal acts—acts whose origin has been traced back at least to Roman times. On the stage, one of the great fascinations of such innocent melodramas of the nineteenth century as *Uncle*

1

Tom's Cabin was the opportunity to see animals on stage—real bloodhounds chasing Little Eva across the ice floes, for example. But even such exalted showplaces as the Metropolitan Opera cannot resist the temptation to bring an animal onstage; in the Met's production of the Russian opera *Boris Gudonov,* the tenor makes a rather nervous appearance on horseback. Somehow, there is something in an animal that appeals to a basic instinct in human beings.

Given that basic appeal and the old show business tradition, it is only natural that animals should be really big in the movies. From the earliest days, some of the greatest screen stars have been nonhuman. Almost every animal on earth, starting with the dog and the horse and running over to the rat and the ant, has played a starring role in one movie or another. And, not content with the animals that nature has provided, moviemakers in the United States and elsewhere have created a whole imaginary menagerie of animal stars —with such success that the make-believe animals often take on lives of their own; fans argue impassionedly about the relative merits of King Kong and Godzilla, or balance the appeal of Mickey Mouse against that of Bugs Bunny.

Movies have several advantages over other forms of show business, when it comes to presenting animals. The opportunity of inventing new kinds of animals is unique to film. Would you like a fifty-foot ape? Or a mule that can talk? Or a horse that can fly? A llama with a head at each end? A giant, city-destroying octopus? A flock of winged monkeys? Just ask the special-features department, and it will produce these and other wonders on film.

For the filmmaker who wants to stay with real animals, film offers other advantages. On the stage or in the circus, a performing animal has to get a trick right every time. In the movies, the animal can do the trick over and over until it gets it just right. Film also allows the use of stand-ins for animals, so that three or four look-alikes can be used in a single animal role. And special film techniques ranging from double exposure to the use of models can give animals on film abilities that they never have in real life.

That sort of film trickery with animals began in the earliest days of the movies. When the famous director D. W. Griffith was a young and struggling actor, the first movie in which he appeared was *Rescued from an Eagle's Nest*, made in 1908, which had a fierce-looking eagle (not very convincing to today's trained eye but apparently impressive to audiences of that era) picking up a baby and flying away with it— something, incidentally, which a real eagle would never do. (Griffith played a woodcutter who rescued the child.)

At the very beginning, the movies faked their wild animals. Someone would slip into a lion's skin or a gorilla suit as the need arose; often, the director would use an empty animal skin. But as audiences became more sophisticated, some filmmakers began to collect animals. Mack Sennett, the king of slapstick comedy, had one of the largest menageries in the early days of Hollywood. One of Sennett's stars was a cat named Pepper, whose abilities included enough willpower to avoid eating a mouse when the script called for both to appear in the same scene. There was a horse named Butterfly, skilled at stunts—riding off a roof, for instance. There were several Great Danes, including one named Teddy who was valuable enough to rate a double for dangerous scenes. In a movie titled *The Extra Girl*, starring the great Mabel Normand, Teddy played a big scene in which he put up a fight against being sewed into a lion suit. That scene led, naturally, to a later confrontation in which Mabel Normand mistook a real lion for the fake. The real lion came from Sennett's collection; the stars in Sennett's pride of lions included beasts named Duke and Numa, who could be counted on to follow their trainers' instructions without getting the urge for an early meal when they were on the set with human actors.

Sennett was interested in animals primarily for slapstick possibilities; one of his dog stars, Cameo, could smoke cigars and drink gin. Other moviemakers got interested in animals for their own sake. When former President Theodore Roosevelt went off to Africa on a well-publicized safari in 1908, he was surprised on his return to find that theaters were showing what were advertised as films of his hunting exploits. A Chicago producer named William Selig had bought an old lion, dressed some local inhabitants in African costumes, turned a corner of his studio into a "jungle" and had made his own version of the safari. Selig went on to film a serial called *The Adventures of Kathlyn,* in which the heroine was pursued by lions, tigers, and other wild beasts, escaping narrowly each week so that the next chase and escape could begin.

Selig had competition from the Vitagraph studio, which was buying up wild animals at a great clip. One of Vitagraph's early efforts was a film called *Wild Animals at Large,* which featured a train wreck that freed all the animals of a traveling circus. The studio had fenced off a ten-acre site in New Jersey for the film, but its plans went awry when a leopard got over the fence and wandered into a nearby village. A customer in a barbershop was petrified to find the leopard clawing at his trousers. Although the man was not badly hurt, he sued the studio, claiming that his hair had turned white and fallen out because of the encounter. The studio settled for $3,000, an enormous sum in those days. Vitagraph turned the incident to its own account by writing the scene into the script, but after that incident the studio had no great heart for further animal epics.

Selig, meanwhile, had found that making movies about animals was less profitable than supplying animals to other studios who wanted them for movies. He went into what has, ever since, been a thriving line of work, raising and training every species of animal that Hollywood producers could desire. He was only one of a number of animal providers and trainers who have flourished in the movie business. When Hollywood has needed an animal, someone has always been ready to supply it.

Sometimes the orders are for animals in miscellaneous types and numbers: a dozen bullfrogs, a swarm of bees, a few white mice, a herd of cattle, a bunch of horses for a Western. Sometimes the filmmakers' wants are exotic: a tarantula, an iguana, a boa constrictor, a turtle. That sort of order, in which no special skill is needed, is relatively easy to fill (although the animal suppliers sometimes must literally beat the bushes for snakes or insects). The fun begins when the filmmaker needs something special from an animal.

It's easy for a writer to create a role in which a leopard is a comfortably tame pet (as in the Katharine Hepburn-Cary Grant comedy *Bringing Up Baby*) or one in which a human trains rats to carry out all his orders (as in the 1971 thriller *Willard*) or one in which a smart cat inherits a whole baseball team (as in the 1951 comedy *Rhubarb*). Getting the animals to do everything that's written into the script is something else. Some animals, including most birds, are literally untrainable. Some can be trained to perform a limited repertory of tricks by the judicious use of food as a reward. Some can be made to appear to be doing the unusual with the help of the special effects that are possible only in the movies. Sometimes a whole bunch of animals can be used to produce the effects required for one role; in *Rhubarb*, the feline star of the film had the staggering total of twenty-two stand-ins.

But every once in a while, the animal equivalent of a genius comes along—an animal that can be trained to do things that aren't possible for most other animals. When such an animal is discovered, legends can begin and fortunes can be made. Usually, a collaboration is required between the animal and the trainer: animals respond best when they get understanding treatment, and the ability to train animals is an art, not a science. But even the best trainer can't make an animal into a star unless the animal has the same indefinable star quality that singles out human actors as stars.

For example, the original Lassie started what turned out to be an entertainment dynasty with a single scene in 1942. Metro-Goldwyn-Mayer Studios was filming *Lassie Come Home.* It was late summer, the time of year when collies shed their coats. Female collies shed more heavily than males, so the female dog that had been cast in the title role didn't look good enough for the part. Animal trainer Rudd Weatherwax, who was well known in Hollywood, had a male collie named Pal, who was originally hired as a double for the star. When the female shed her coat, Pal was quickly inserted into the star role.

The crucial event came in a scene in which Lassie had to swim across the roaring river. Pal swam as instructed—and then added a touch that couldn't have been anticipated. When he came out of the river, Pal didn't shake himself off as most dogs would. Instead,

The Magic of Lassie
An old canine trouper meets an old human trouper, James Stewart. (Wrather, 1978)

the collie walked a few steps and then dropped, as with exhaustion. In a line that is reminiscent of many a Broadway melodrama, director Fred Wilcox is said to have told Weatherwax, "Rudd, Pal went into the river, but Lassie came out."

Hollywood's animal history is speckled with such stories, which are the animal equivalents of that old chestnut about a human movie star being discovered in a drug store by a talent scout. But there's one difference between human star quality and that of animals: with animals, stardom can be handed on from generation to generation. Indeed, that is a necessity, because animals are short-lived by human standards. The trainer with an animal star is wise to start the search for a successor quickly—and to waste no time finding the successor to the successor. What can't be provided by natural star quality in an animal can be provided by good training, which insures the continuation of a dynasty. Lassie represents one of the longest of such Hollywood dynasties. By 1979, it was in its fifth generation, being passed on from father to son. Rudd Weatherwax was still the trainer.

The Lassie dynasty has produced seven feature films, a television series that ran nineteen years, and a long series of commercial endorsements—including one for, of course, dog food. It is all testimony to one of the enduring truths of show business: people love animals. And being a business, show business gives people what they want.

Chapter Two

THE GREAT DOG STARS

Some twelve thousand years ago, in what is now the Jordan Valley of Israel, a middle-aged man of the Natufian civilization died. When modern archaeologists excavated his tomb, they found that he had been buried with one hand lying gently on a puppy that had been buried with him. According to the archaeologists, that tomb shows that the very first animal domesticated by the human race was the dog, which was mankind's hunting companion and pet even before humans began making use of such food animals as pigs and cattle.

Given that long bond of affection between humans and dogs, it is only natural that most of the great animal stars of the movies have been dogs. One of the greatest of those stars was a German shepherd who is almost forgotten now but was one of the big money-makers of the 1920s: a dog named Strongheart.

Strongheart started as an idea in the mind of a husband-and-wife team, movie writer Jane Murfin and director Larry Trimble, who decided in 1920 that a series of films starring a heroic dog would be a profitable venture. As they told the story later, they looked at hundreds of candidates for the role without finding a dog that met their requirements. After exhausting the possibilities in the United States, they continued their talent hunt in Europe.

And there, the story continues, they met a three-year-old German shepherd named Etzel von Oeringen, born of champion stock in Germany and trained to kill for military purposes. In the dramatic fashion that one would expect of a Hollywood saga, the Americans decided that they could tame this animal who kept his very handlers in constant fear. Naturally, they succeeded, although insisting that their methods would forever remain secret.

Etzel von Oeringen, now named Strongheart, achieved stardom in a 1921 epic titled *The Silent Call*. Strongheart played a dog that was half wolf and that was noticeably more intelligent than its human owners. In the course of the plot, Strongheart saved the life of the heroine and managed to get her safely married, all while raising a family of his own, born of a marriage with a she-wolf. But Strongheart's family was doomed to tragedy. There was a scene in which Strongheart returns to their cave to find that an explosion has sealed off his puppies; a scene that brought tears to many an eye and established Strongheart's box office appeal.

Soon Strongheart was answering numerous letters by sending pictures that were autographed with a paw print. He even inspired a book, *Letters to Strongheart,* in which the writer said that the dog "rose above and dominated the story, the members of the cast, the production, and even the scenery."

But Strongheart soon lost first place in the public's affection to a dog who still remains an instantly recognizable Hollywood legend, even though few of today's fans have ever seen one of his films: Rin Tin Tin.

Quite fittingly, Rin Tin Tin was discovered in even more dramatic fashion than Strongheart. The Rin Tin Tin story began during World War I when Lee Duncan, a noncommissioned pilot in the American Air Force, heard some pitiful whines as he was inspecting a newly captured German airport in France. Duncan found a litter of German shepherd pups huddled with their mother in a trench. He gave away some pups, but kept two for himself, a male and a female whom he named Nenette and Rin Tin Tin after knitted good-luck charms which were carried by the French during the war. (The original Nenette and Rin Tin Tin supposedly were human lovers who were the only survivors of a German bombing raid on a crowded railroad station.)

When the war ended, Duncan brought the dogs home with him. Nenette died, but Duncan began

Rin Tin Tin shows off one of his skills for a publicity shot.

training Rin Tin Tin on his ranch in Southern California. For several years, Duncan's efforts to break into movies got nowhere. Then, in 1925, he persuaded the then-struggling movie studio called Warner Brothers to make a picture based on a short story called "Llewellyn and His Dog." Warners hired an unknown writer named Darryl Zanuck to turn out a script for a silent film that was titled *Where the North Begins.* As they say in Hollywood, the rest is history.

After Rin Tin Tin arrived, Warners struggled no more. Such films as *The Night Cry, Clash of Wolves,* and *A Dog of the Regiment* might have predictable plots, but film audiences loved to see Rin Tin Tin go through his paces. When Rinty, as he was popularly called, died in 1932, he got a newspaper obituary that is memorable: "Rin Tin Tin, greatest of the animal motion picture actors, pursued a ghostly villain into a canine happy hunting grounds today. More than eighty years old as comparative human age is measured, his passing was mourned this morning by his owner and friend, Lee Duncan."

Needless to say, Rinty II was waiting in the wings. The second Rin Tin Tin did not have the success that his father did, and there was even a marvelously malicious bit of Hollywood gossip of the times to explain why. Sound films had just come in, and there were whispers that Rin Tin Tin II had a squeaky bark that could not match his father's full-throated roar. The gossips even said that the bark of Rinty II was actually done by a human actor and then dubbed into the sound track—a rumor that was denied indignantly by Duncan.

But the dynasty rolled on, achieving some impressive results. Rin Tin Tin III not only starred in films but also served in the military during World War II, training dogs for the K-9 Corps. Rinty III held the rank of sergeant and was given several medals, including a Purple Heart that was awarded for an injury he suffered when a jeep ran over his leg during maneuvers. Duncan rated Rinty III as good an actor as his grandfather. He could respond to more than five hundred commands—crawling like a panther, feigning sleep, fighting imaginary fleas (for a comic effect), pulling a bell rope, herding sheep and chickens, beating out a fire with a sack, and simulating a vicious attack on wrong-doers, to mention just a few of his accomplishments.

When the television era arrived, the Rin Tin Tin dynasty was ready. Rinty IV, born on January 18, 1956, in an air-conditioned kennel on Duncan's California ranch, starred in a long-running television series, "The Adventures of Rin Tin Tin," that was close to the top of the ratings in the late 1960s. (The plot had Rinty serving with the U. S. Cavalry out West during frontier days.)

To measure how far Duncan and Rin Tin Tin had come since the humble beginnings, Rinty IV carried a $250,000 life insurance policy, was protected by five guard dogs, lived in air-conditioned comfort, and ate a carefully chosen diet which included beef that came

exclusively from registered cattle. When Warners celebrated its thirtieth anniversary, Rin Tin Tin was at the
head table, and the Rinty dynasty could look back on
a career of stardom with many of Hollywood's biggest
names, including Myrna Loy, Jackie Cooper, and
George Brent, in films, series, and TV programs that
had earned literally hundreds of millions of dollars.

Even before Rin Tin Tin faded from the Hollywood
scene, Lassie came along, as if to prove that Hollywood always needs at least one big dog star. To
merely run down the list of the human stars in the
first Lassie film, *Lassie Come Home,* is to demonstrate
why actors dislike appearing in animal movies: the
animal always steals the scene. *Lassie Come Home*
had a cast that included such unquestioned stars and
stars to be as Elizabeth Taylor (making her first film
appearance), Roddy McDowall, Edmund Gwenn,
Dame May Whitty, and Elsa Lanchester. All that most
people remember about the film these days is Lassie
coming home, over hill and dale, against all the odds,
in a plot that had the dog returning to its original
owners after they had been forced to sell it far, far
away.

Rudd Weatherwax, Lassie's trainer, was no Hollywood novice. Weatherwax, who grew up in Los Angeles, was working in the movies in his early teens.
When he was sixteen, he went to work for Henry
East, a trainer who supplied many dogs for bit parts
on the screen. Before Lassie came along, Weatherwax
trained a number of dogs who earned a good measure

of fame in the movies. One of them was Asta, a wire-haired terrier who appeared with William Powell and Myrna Loy in the "Thin Man" series of detective comedies in the 1930s and 1940s.

For those who love motion picture trivia, Asta is a double delight. Beginners can earn a point or two in a trivia contest simply by recalling the name of the dog. More advanced trivia buffs can display their knowledge by pointing out that in the first film of the series, *The Thin Man* (1934), based on a Dashiell Hammett story, the Thin Man was one of the victims, not the detective; in later films, the Thin Man tag stuck to William Powell. (Really advanced trivia practitioners can name the dog who starred in the Blondie series of comedies. It was Daisy, who was also trained by Weatherwax.)

In 1940, shortly after Weatherwax and his brother had opened a kennel and training school, a customer brought in a young, difficult collie named Pal, hoping the dog could be broken of the habit of barking too much. The customer then decided that he'd rather not have the dog, and Weatherwax kept it. Again, as they are fond of saying in Hollywood, the rest is history.

Lassie Come Home was followed by—what else—*Son of Lassie*, released in 1945, which involved Lassie in some World War II adventures. Then came *Courage of Lassie* (1946), a film that brought back Elizabeth Taylor as the dog's owner and also featured that grand old trouper, Frank Morgan (who is best remembered because he played the Wizard of Oz in the

Judy Garland film); this time the plot centered around Elizabeth's efforts to reform Lassie, who had been turned into a killer dog by military training. *The Hills of Home* (1948) put Lassie in Scotland, opposite Edmund Gwenn, and *The Sun Comes Up* (1949) is notable because it was the last film appearance of Jeanette MacDonald (famous for film musicals with Nelson Eddy), who played an embittered widow who was humanized by Lassie and his young owner, Claude Jarman, Jr. *Challenge of Lassie* (1950), which again featured Edmund Gwenn, turned out to be the last Lassie film for a long time.

All the Lassie films made money for MGM, but the one-a-year pace was beginning to make the formula wear thin. MGM lost interest in Lassie and dropped the dog from its roster of stars ("More Stars Than There Are in the Heavens" was the motto of MGM, which was then at the top of the heap in Hollywood). The studio turned over all the rights in Lassie's name and material to Weatherwax, in settlement of some money that was owed to him. The agreement looked like a bad deal for Weatherwax at the time, but it turned out to be a gold mine. Television was on the horizon, and it soon became evident that Lassie was a TV natural.

Lassie had briefly starred in a radio serial, but a bark was no substitute for the whole animal. The Lassie television series went on the air in September 1954 and lasted in one form or another for the next nineteen years. Even after the producers stopped filming new episodes, reruns continued for several more years. Lassie's television popularity was great enough to prompt another feature film, *The Magic of Lassie*, which appeared in 1978, featuring such stars as James Stewart, Mickey Rooney, and Alice Faye, with Debby Boone singing a few songs—but, unfortunately, it was not a box-office success.

But it wasn't the dog's fault. The star of the film, the great-great-great granddaughter of the original, got good notices; it was the rest of the film that the critics didn't like.

Just to show that the appeal of movie dogs hadn't worn off, along came a new star, Benji. Again, there was a touch of romance in the beginnings of this dog star. Unlike Rin Tin Tin and Lassie, Benji is a mongrel who was found in the Burbank, California, animal shelter, and who is described vaguely as a mixture of cocker spaniel, poodle, and schnauzer. Like many others of today's film stars, Benji started off in television, playing for seven years on the series "Petticoat Junction."

Until 1973, Benji's name was Higgins. Then producer Joe Camp went looking for a dog to star in a film that, he said, would look at the world from the animal's point of view. Camp found Higgins at the animal farm of trainer Frank Inn. The dog was renamed after Camp's Yorkshire terrier and made the movie, which earned an impressive $45 million at the box office. Benji's show-business training helped to earn that money; to promote the film, he visited sixty-

Benji
Benji and a friend. (Mulberry Square, 1973)

four cities, making as many as eight appearances in a day.

When the time came for the inevitable sequel, *For the Love of Benji*, there was one problem: the original Benji was a very old dog, aged thirteen or fourteen when the first film was made, and was now ready for retirement (at last report he was living out a comfortable old age with the best of food and care). The part was taken over by Benji Two, who not only had the father's looks but also the ability to work for the camera. It happened that Benji Two was a female, but as the story of Lassie shows, sex is a trivial consideration for movie animals.

For the Love of Benji was another hit, and Benji was a star, commanding $7,500 for personal appearances and appearing in what the ABC television network described as the first prime-time special to headline an animal, *The Phenomenon of Benji*, which was aired in 1978—and which led to *Benji's Very Own Christmas Story* later that year.

By this time, Benji had come a long way from the mongrel life. He traveled first-class on airplanes, was doused with perfume when he made personal appearances, was awarded with cubes of filet mignon, with the grease carefully strained out, for doing his tricks (opening a mailbox and taking out a letter, yawning or sneezing on command, and much more complicated things for the screen), and sometimes dined out at excellent restaurants with his trainer. And just to show the continuity of the movie-animal business, Benji's trainer Frank Inn once worked with Rudd Weatherwax, and Benji was the second dog to make the Animal Actors Hall of Fame; the first was Lassie.

Among them, Rin Tin Tin, Lassie, and Benji sum up the image of the ideal movie dog. Benji is lovable.

Lassie is wise and lovable. Rin Tin Tin is strong, wise, and lovable. None of them has any of the annoying traits of real-life dogs—chewing the legs of furniture, for example, or taking a nip at the hand of an unwary child. When a movie dog is accused of biting someone, the accusation usually is false and/or malicious, and it usually leads to some heart-warming plot developments. A prime example is the accusation against Toto, Dorothy's dog in *The Wizard of Oz*. Dorothy runs away to save Toto from being destroyed by the nasty Miss Gulch and, because of this, is carried away to the magical land of Oz by a tornado. No Toto, no story.

The nobility of movie dogs can be overplayed. In the television series, Lassie spent most of her time out in the woods, protecting small, defenseless animals from wolves, cougars, and other predators. Critics complained that this sort of story was giving viewers a false picture of the real world, where a predator is not doing anything evil when it sets out to hunt for a meal. The critics added that Lassie herself was no vegetarian, and thus would have to be doing some hunting on her own to survive in the woods. "What do they think she is eating out there?" growled one commentator. "Canned dog food?"

Nevertheless, the image lives on. There is an occasional spoof, such as *Won Ton Ton*, the mildly successful 1975 comedy that got laughs simply by having its animal hero carry every feat of Rin Tin Tin just one step too far. But the real box-office bucks are made by those who take their dog heroes seriously—a fact that has been grasped firmly by the Walt Disney organization.

Disney dog films include *Greyfriars' Bobby* (1960), based on the story of a terrier who mourns for years at his master's grave; *Big Red* (1961), about an Irish setter who is noble and brave beyond belief; and *Old Yeller* (1957), about a lovable but tough mongrel who fought to protect a homesteading family in Texas. The list of movie dog stars is almost endless, from Pete the Pup of the *Our Gang* comedy series to Buck, the huge half wolf of the 1935 film version of Jack London's *Call of the Wild;* to Mr. Smith, who nearly stole a 1937 comedy, *The Awful Truth,* from Cary Grant and Irene Dunne, its human stars; to Sam, John Wayne's faithful sidekick in the 1953 Western, *Hondo;* to . . . but name your own favorite. The twelve-thousand-year-old partnership between humans and dogs is strong enough to provide innumerable variations on the eternal theme.

Chapter Three

HORSE HEROES

The story goes that when Marilyn Monroe was about to begin a Western role at the beginning of her film career, she was warned that her costar was a notorious scene-stealer. "It's not him that worries me," she said. "It's those hammy horses."

Any animal that could get Marilyn Monroe worried is certainly worth careful consideration. It's true that in the history of the movie business, horses have ranked just behind dogs as film stars. But a word of explanation is needed for today's generation of filmgoers, because they might require an introduction to a whole chapter of film history that now is concluded.

Traditionally, the movie horse has not been able to achieve stardom on his own. With a few exceptions, the great movie horses have been the partners of the great movie cowboys. And for half a century, the cowboy was one of the pillars of the motion picture business. Starting with "Bronco Billy" Anderson in 1909, Hollywood featured a long series of Western stars who made movie after movie. Even though the plots hardly varied, the public never tired of seeing cowboy heroes best the bad guys. Almost every one of those cowboy heroes had a horse who came close to being a costar. The cowboy's horse was traditionally intelligent enough to carry complicated messages, brave enough to save people from any given hazard, faithful enough to smell out the bad guys, and sturdy enough to gallop all day without tiring.

Unhappily, the tradition of the Hollywood cowboy and his horse came to an abrupt end when the television era began. Most Westerns were made to be shown as the second film of a double feature. But the double feature died when television arrived. Instead of going out to the movies, viewers began staying home to watch television. Hollywood could no longer turn out huge numbers of movies; instead, it began making a small number of blockbuster films, designed to lure people away from the free entertainment offered by the tube at home. There was a brief period when television showed old movie Westerns in prime time—Hopalong Cassidy enjoyed a moment of fame—but that faded quickly. Today, there are any number of old Westerns resting in film vaults, untouched and unwanted by today's audiences.

And so one has to remind film fans of the fame once enjoyed by such stars as William S. Hart, who came riding on to the screen on his celebrated horse Fritz. Bill Hart and Fritz established the standard Hollywood horse story in all of its decorative details. Fritz was a pinto who was described as being absolutely fearless (on command, it was said, he rode through a plate-glass window), having a sense of humor, sulking when his master left him for a few days, and responding like a human when Bill talked to him. If there was a good deal of embroidery in the fabric, the public was willing to accept it.

The man-and-his-horse legend reached giant proportions with the arrival of Tom Mix, who, unlike the Eastern-bred Hart, was a real cowboy. Tom Mix had two wonder horses, Old Blue and Tony, as well as a Great Dane named Duke. It was hard to separate the kernel of truth from the colorful publicity stories that were told about Mix; he was supposed to have taken part in the Spanish-American War, the Boxer Rebellion in China, and the Boer War, to have suffered innumerable wounds and broken bones, and to have served as a sheriff out West before being discovered by the movies. Maybe, maybe not. But Mix certainly was a tough, gritty actor. He insisted on doing most of his own stunts, in the course of which he suffered a number of severe injuries.

Old Blue died not long after Mix's film career began in 1910. Tony kept going for many years, living to the ripe old age of thirty-four. One reason for Tony's longevity was the ample use of doubles. Although the public was never told about it, there actu-

Tom Mix and his favorite movie horse, Tony.

ally were three or four "Tonys"; the real one was spared the more hazardous stunts and was reserved for use in scenes where he could perform his repertory of tricks, such as untying a knot with his teeth.

Tom Mix went out when talking pictures came in; his voice just wasn't good enough. But the golden era of movie Westerns was just beginning. Every studio seemed to have its Western star, and every Western star had his wonder horse. There was Tex Maynard and his horse Tarzan; Tex Ritter and Flash; Bill Elliott and Thunder; Hopalong Cassidy (dressed entirely in black) and his white horse Topper; Gene Autry and his horse Champion.

And there was Roy Rogers, the "King of the Cowboys," and his wonder horse Trigger. Like Gene Autry, Roy Rogers was a new kind of Western star; he sang. In fact, Rogers, again like Autry, started as a Country and Western singer, forming the Sons of the Pioneers singing group which appeared in his films. A typical Roy Rogers Western was set in a never-never land where the hero lived on a ranch but was always immaculately dressed and spent more of his time strumming his guitar at a bonfire than working on the range. It was quite a change from the two-fisted days of Tom Mix.

The one thing that hadn't changed was the important role of the cowboy's best friend, his horse. Trigger was a golden palamino who eventually appeared in eighty-seven movies and more than a hundred episodes of the Roy Rogers television show, which had its run early in the 1950s. (After TV, Rogers spent years on the rodeo tour.) Although Trigger had two doubles in later years, Rogers insisted that he always rode the original Trigger in all his films.

When Trigger died at the age of thirty-three in 1966, his obituary got the same display as that of many a human star. Instead of burying the horse, Rogers had Trigger stuffed and mounted for display. "It really shook me up when Trigger passed on," Rogers told one reporter. "It was like losing one of the family. He was beautifully trained. I could do anything with him. When I'd come to the barn or the corral, he'd nuzzle me and hope for a lump of sugar. They threw away the pattern when they made Trigger. During all those hard rides for pictures and television, he never fell once. We had to do more retakes for human actors than for Trigger."

That last remark is a good explanation of star quality in an animal. Most animals can learn to do a few tricks. To achieve stardom, an animal must be able to learn new tricks quickly and to respond to subtle and complicated commands, often given by hand signal. Veteran animal trainers swear that an animal star such as Trigger or Champion can think almost in the way that a human does. When a trainer comes across such an animal, the result can be a fortune.

Only a few horses have made it. In the early days there was Rex, "King of the Wild Horses," the first horse to be given star billing on his own. Later there was Fury, who played the title role in several movies,

Trigger shows off the talents that made him so beloved by Roy Rogers.

including one of the many versions of the classic children's story *Black Beauty* and a 1954 film titled *The Gypsy Colt* (the plot, which might sound familiar, had the horse finding its way home after its masters had sold it far away). Fury even had his own television series for a time; it was a period in the 1950s when television was getting its usual criticism for giving children too much sex and violence, and when the Lassie show had demonstrated that clean family entertainment could sell soap flakes and breakfast cereals.

Fury could not only limp, kneel, "grin," lie down, and obey signals telling him to go left or right; he could also play dead, untie ropes, and retrieve on command. More important than this set repertory was Fury's ability to learn special routines after only a brief rehearsal. In one film, for example, Fury had to chase a fleeing ranch hand and kick a package out of his hand without hurting him. He mastered the demanding stunt after two run-throughs.

"I've never known an animal like Fury," his trainer Ralph McCutcheon told a reporter. "All of us have known animals who are smart, but what makes Fury different is an amazing aptitude. We rehearse a new bit twice and are ready for a take."

At the other end of the spectrum are the ordinary Hollywood horses, the anonymous animals that the posse would mount when they set off to chase the bank robbers. At a time when Fury was getting $40,000 a picture, the going price for saddle horses in Westerns was $7.50 to $10 a day. In the boom days of the Hollywood Western, hundreds of these horses were needed, and the animals often did not have an easy time of it. When the script called for the hero to jump from a balcony onto the back of a galloping horse, the hero—or a stunt man—would do exactly that. The 1976 film *Hearts of the West,* which spoofed the early Westerns, made fun of the pain that Beau Bridges experienced when he performed that stunt, but the movie paid no attention to what the horse must have felt.

Humane society officials have moved in to stop most of the worst practices. Stunt men aren't happy about it much of the time. *Hooper,* a 1977 film in which Burt Reynolds played a stunt man, gave an accurate representation of the stunt man's point of view. In one scene in which Reynolds was to take a hundred-foot dive, the humane society official was pictured as being more concerned about the dog that Reynolds was supposed to take with him than with the safety of the man.

Still, changes have come. In the old days of Westerns, when the script called for a horse to fall down at the gallop, the common practice was to use a "Running W": a band around the horse's belly, with a cable attached by rings to the horse's front legs. When the cable is tightened, the horse's legs are pulled up and it goes down. Stunt men insist that the Running W doesn't hurt a horse, and that the man who takes the fall runs all of the risk. Nevertheless, the Running W got into bad repute because of the damage it could do in inexperienced or careless hands. Falls now are done using horses that have been specially trained to go down on command.

Aside from the classic Western, the standard Hollywood horse story used to team a boy and a colt. Oversimplifying, there were two basic plots: either the boy was in danger of losing the colt (something heartwarming always happened in the end to prevent the loss) or the boy trained the colt to be a prizewinning racehorse. The most outstanding version of the second plot was *National Velvet* (1944), which had a girl rather than a boy doing the work. The girl was Elizabeth Taylor, then a child star, who was fresh from her work with Lassie and who rode her horse to victory in England's Grand National race with the help of trainer Mickey Rooney. One of the best versions of the first standard plot was *My Friend Flicka* (1943), which had Roddy McDowall taming a rebellious stallion out West.

My Friend Flicka was successful enough to prompt a sequel, *Thunderhead, Son of Flicka* (1945). In later years, McDowall said that while he enjoyed working with Lassie in *Lassie Come Home,* the horse pictures were far from pleasant. While Lassie was a real trouper, Flicka wasn't. In fact, a total of six horses were needed to play Flicka (there were nine Thunderheads), and the main Flicka had a mean streak and kept trying to step on McDowall's feet.

Alas, the standard boy-and-his-horse film fell out of favor as Hollywood's days of innocence passed and

My Friend Flicka
*A boy, his dad, and his horse: Roddy McDowall and Preston
Foster with Flicka. (20th Century-Fox, 1943)*

FACING PAGE:
National Velvet
*The cast includes Butch Jenkins, Elizabeth Taylor, a horse
named Pie, and a man named Mickey Rooney. (MGM,
1944)*

producers discovered the box-office potential of sex, violence, and profanity. For a time in the late 1970s, it seemed as if the horse film was making a comeback. In 1978, Columbia spent a lot of money on *Casey's Shadow*, with Walter Matthau and Alexis Smith, and MGM released *International Velvet*, a somewhat delayed sequel to *National Velvet*, starring a teenaged Tatum O'Neal. Both used Plot B, with mild variations. In *Casey's Shadow*, the horse was trained for quarter racing, while in *International Velvet*, the horse is trained for equestrian competition in the Olympics.

Both films flopped at the box office. Apparently, something had changed in the movies. The big horse picture of 1978 was *Equus*, a psychiatric drama about a boy undergoing analysis because he blinds horses. And when NBC remade that old reliable, *Black Beauty*, as a five-part series in 1978, not much of the original plot survived. One critic complained that TV saw *Black Beauty* "not as a tract on behalf of gentleness toward animals great and small, but as a pretext for trotting out a pack of neurotic adults who suffer and squabble and cough while a disinterested horse watches from the corner."

But none of this should be taken to mean that the old horse movie is gone forever. The old basic appeal is still there, waiting to be tapped by someone who has a good hand with the tried-and-true formulas. After all, who would argue with Marilyn Monroe?

Chapter Four

THE BEAST IN
THE JUNGLE

From the beginning, Hollywood has been fascinated by wild beasts—elephants, tigers, lions, apes, rhinos, and any other species that could be worked into a film. But very little of Hollywood's adventures with wildlife have had much connection with the real thing. Filmmakers generally swing to one extreme or another: either they make wild animals seem tamer than they are or they make them seem wilder than they are.

Two species who have gotten bad reputations because of the latter habit are the gorilla and the wolf. Until recently, the movies have pictured both as villains of the worst dye. It is part of movie folklore that gorillas are vicious animals, dangerous whenever they are encountered, always ready to attack humans, and consistently displaying a mean streak. As for wolves, it is an equally old movie tradition that they are utterly savage killers who have no redeeming qualities and who destroy other animals and attack humans out of sheer blood lust.

Hollywood can hardly be blamed for these attitudes, since they reflect an old, established image of both species. It is only in relatively recent years that ethologists—scientists who study animals in their native environments—have made a concerted effort to change the old images because of observations in the wild.

Those observations have shown that the gorilla is a gentle animal who eats only vegetation, avoids contact with humans whenever possible, and poses no threat unless it is attacked. The breast-beating and roaring that seem so ferocious are actually just an effort by the gorilla to scare possible attackers away by a bluff. In addition, the gorilla is also one of the most intelligent animals known; a captive gorilla named Koko has been taught dozens of words (which are "spoken" by sign language) and is estimated to have an intelligence quotient of 60 to 90.

As for the wolf, observers describe it as an animal that is no more vicious than any other predator, that does not attack humans unless provoked, and that has strong family ties. Rather than being a totally destructive killer, the wolf is described, by scientists who have studied its behavior, as a useful creature who helps to maintain the strength of the species on which it preys because it kills only the animals that are least equipped to survive.

Nevertheless, the old snarling image of the wolf is so well established in the movies that it is difficult to see how it will ever be erased, no matter how false it may be. And at the other end of the spectrum, some equally false pictures of wild animals as jolly, good-humored pets have been firmly—and just as mistakenly—established by filmmakers.

A prime example of an animal that has benefited from an unintentional movie public-relations campaign is the chimpanzee. Just as Hollywood started with the preconception of a gorilla as a man-killer, so the moviemakers began with the belief that a chimp is a harmless, fun-loving animal who makes an ideal pet. That image was established primarily by the Tarzan movies, which featured a jungle family with a remarkable similarity to the typical suburban family of a television situation comedy. There was Tarzan, born an English lord but reared by apes in the jungle; his well-spoken wife, Jane; their son, Boy; and their household companion, Cheetah the chimpanzee. In most of the Tarzan movies—the best were made in the 1930s and 1940s and starred Olympic swimmer Johnny Weissmuller as Tarzan and Maureen O'Sullivan as Jane—Cheetah was very much a member of the family.

When the family was peacefully at home, Cheetah would gambol, turn somersaults, clap hands, and in general act the cheery clown. In times of peril, Cheetah was always available to carry messages, untie knots, and perform whatever other semihuman chores were demanded by the script. Throughout the Tarzan series, Cheetah was always a cuddly armful who wouldn't harm a child.

The reality was something else. A chimpanzee is not vicious, but it is definitely a wild animal whose behavior becomes increasingly unpredictable as it grows older. The image of Cheetah the gentle pet was maintained only by using a series of chimps, each of whom was replaced when it became necessary. The first in the line was a chimpanzee named Joe Martin, who appeared opposite the first screen Tarzan, Elmo Lincoln, in a 1918 film called *Romance of Tarzan*. (That film was, incidentally, the second to be made. The first was *Tarzan of the Apes*, also starring Elmo Lincoln, which appeared earlier in 1918.)

Joe Martin made many film appearances but eventually grew too big and too unpredictable for films. He was sold to a circus. Other chimpanzees followed as the series rolled along through what eventually totaled thirty-six feature films, four serials, a radio series in the 1930s, and a television series in the 1960s. (All were based on the Tarzan books, written by Edgar Rice Burroughs, who readily acknowledged that he had never been in Africa when he wrote about jungle life.)

Toward the end, Cheetah was given smaller and smaller roles. Rather symbolically, one of the last chimps to play Cheetah came to a decidedly unjolly end in 1957. The chimpanzee, in pain during an illness, broke out of his cage and attacked his trainer as

One big happy family: Cheetah, Johnny Sheffield, Johnny Weissmuller, and Maureen O'Sullivan pose in a studio jungle setting of the Tarzan series.

a posse tried to recapture the animal. When the chimpanzee broke loose and lumbered toward some children who were watching the scene, sheriff's deputies shot it dead.

None of this means that a chimpanzee is a violent animal. It just means that a chimpanzee, like a gorilla, is unpredictable when it is in an unnatural environment. It also means that a chimpanzee, being a wild animal, can't be judged by human standards: behavior that is suitable for a human cannot be expected from an animal. However, Hollywood has persistently tried to give animals human qualities because the customers want it that way. Even when an animal bears no resemblance to a human, its behavior still tends to be judged by human standards in the movies.

The case of the image of the lion in the movies shows how Hollywood can picture animal behavior to meet film needs. One persistent image of the lion is that of a menacing but basically harmless comic figure. In his slapstick comedies, Mack Sennett loved to introduce a lion into a scene for comic effect. Sennett used several lions. One of them was Numa; another, who went on to more than 250 films, was Jackie, who was able to wrestle in apparent play with his trainer, Melvin Koontz.

No one who watches such scenes in the movies should be fooled by what seems to be fun and games. A lion, however tame and well trained, is not to be trusted. It is not uncommon to have someone with a gun standing by, ready to shoot the animal if it should turn wild without warning. If that should happen—good training and careful preparation usually prevents it—it is not the lion who is to blame. The fault is that of the filmmakers who have put the animal in a false situation to please the audience.

The truth is that Hollywood has a long tradition of not caring much for animals unless it is forced to care by law. In the early days, when supervision was lacking, animals were regarded as expendable. For example, the first Tarzan movie, *Tarzan of the Apes*, had a plot that called for Tarzan to kill a lion. That is exactly what happened. Elmo Lincoln, the actor who played Tarzan, was handed a knife and told to kill an aging lion who had been bought for the movie. After some difficulty, Lincoln stabbed the lion to death and, as called for by the script, put his foot triumphantly on the dead beast—only to jump for his life when the lion emitted a fierce roar. It turned out that the lion was indeed dead and that the roar was the result of the pressure of Lincoln's foot, which had expelled the air from the beast's lungs.

The provision of lions and other wild beasts for films became a profitable business for trainers who operated animal farms around Hollywood. The Tarzan series was a dependable customer. Hardly a Tarzan film went by without Johnny Weissmuller wrestling a lion to the death. In real life, the lion often was made tame by drugs or was stuffed for absolute safety; if necessary, the lion was real but a stunt man doubled for Weissmuller.

The easiest way to get wild animals on the screen was to send someone off to Africa to film the animals there, while the stars of the film stayed in California. The actors and the animals could then be brought together by using one of the process shots developed by skilled technicians. One of the most common techniques was—and is—the back projection, which has the live actors playing their roles in front of a screen on which film that has previously been shot is projected.

There can be pitfalls. When Twentieth Century-Fox was making the African adventure *Stanley and Livingstone* (1939), producer Darryl Zanuck sent a unit to Africa to film the animal scenes. Because Zanuck intended to star Tyrone Power in the film, the unit included a double who resembled Power closely. But while the unit was in Africa, Zanuck borrowed Spencer Tracy from MGM to replace Power. Much of the film shot on location had to be discarded, although the remaining shots of wild animals and African scenes were usable.

The trend in more recent years is to make the film on location. The actors may be uncomfortable, but the results are much more realistic. One of the most rewarding results of that practice was the 1966 movie *Born Free,* which was based on the true story of Joy Adamson, who raised three lion cubs to maturity after their mother had been shot accidentally. When the cubs were full-grown, two of them were sent off to zoos. The third, named Elsa, was trained by Joy

Adamson and her husband, George, to live in the wild.

The film was made in Kenya and starred a husband-and-wife acting team, Bill Travers and Virginia McKenna—and, of course, Elsa, who was really three different lions. The critics loved the film, from the shots of the young lion cubs frolicking around the Adamson house to the scenes in which Elsa slowly learned how to hunt on her own. "There hasn't been as satisfying an ending for the youngsters since Lassie came home," one reviewer said.

But even though the film depicted fact, some animal trickery was needed. One scene called for Elsa to be taken to the seashore, where she learned how to swim. As it happened, Elsa No. 1 in the movie didn't want to swim; the water scenes were made by Elsa No. 2, who usually was a stand-in.

And there were reminders that lions are lions. While working with a cub, Virginia McKenna had a serious accident. One cub playfully knocked her down, and Virginia broke a leg. In a more grim reminder of the gap between movie illusion and reality, one of the lions used in the film was shot and killed when she attacked a human.

The success of *Born Free* led to a sequel, *Living Free,* which reached the screen in 1972 and starred Susan Hampshire and Nigel Davenport. This one followed the fate of Elsa's three cubs in adventures that included encounters with a rhino and a python. The critics complained that the film got tedious before Elsa's

Born Free
Elsa the lioness gets a lesson in hunting from Virginia McKenna and Bill Travers. (Columbia, 1966)

cubs were happily established on a game preserve, but there were no complaints about the fascinating shots of the lions in real African scenes.

For those who don't like lions, Hollywood can always supply elephants. The elephant in films is worth recalling if only because of one line spoken by Jimmy Durante in the 1962 film version of the musical *Jumbo,* which is about a circus with financial troubles. At one point, Durante is stealing away with Jumbo, an elephant whom he is trying to save from the circus's creditors, when he is confronted by a sheriff who asks, "Where do you think you're going with that elephant?"

"Elephant," says Durante, looking around in surprise. "What elephant?"

One actor who started with elephants and never lost his identification with them was Sabu (real name Sabu Dastagir), a star who reached his peak in the 1940s. Sabu was the son of a mahout, or elephant driver, employed by the Maharajah of Mysore. In 1936, the British producer, Sir Alexander Korda, was making *Elephant Boy,* a film based on a tale by Rudyard Kipling, when he came across Sabu. The young Indian boy—he was only twelve years old—had grown up with elephants and was a natural for the role of a tiny lad who could handle the largest pachyderms and was adopted by them when his father died.

Sabu was an instant hit. With white teeth gleaming against his smooth brown skin, his long black hair flowing down his back, Sabu charmed movie audiences. He rode elephants again in *The Jungle Book* (1942), another film based on Kipling's stories, in which he played Mowgli, a boy who was reared by a wolf pack in the jungle. Because World War II was on, the jungle actually was a part of California where Korda had brought together a dense thicket of tropical flowers, trees, and shrubs gathered from estates and nurseries. Audiences thought the scenery (and the wolves, elephants, pythons, bears, cobras, and other animals who were featured in the film) quite real enough. The movie was a hit.

Sabu's real-life story was almost as fascinating as that of the screen characters he played. He was educated at an aristocratic private school in England. When World War II arrived, he went into the U. S. Army Air Force and had a valiant career, winning the Distinguished Flying Cross and other medals. After the war he made a few more animal movies, such as *Man-Eater of Kumaon* (1948) and *Hello, Elephant* (1952), but his career tailed off. He died of a heart attack at the age of thirty-nine.

Typically, when you think of *Elephant Boy*, you think of Sabu, not an elephant, as the star. Elephants are intelligent animals—according to scientists, much more intelligent than dogs or horses—but somehow an elephant never projects much personality on the screen. Perhaps it's a matter of size; an animal as big as a house doesn't come across as a personality. Anyway, movie elephants seem to be memorable as objects, not as subjects. A few elephants come to mind: there

Jungle Boy
Sabu has a ride on his elephant friend, Irawatha. (Korda, 1937)

Hannibal Brooks
Oliver Reed leads his elephant friend toward freedom through the foothills of the Alps. (United Artists, 1969)

is Queenie, who obligingly sprays W. C. Fields with water from her trunk when he wants to take a shower in *You Can't Cheat an Honest Man* (1939). There is the elephant that Michael J. Pollard and Oliver Reed, playing World War II prisoners of war, try to escape with in *Hannibal Brooks* (1969). There is the elephant who provides a happy ending for the pleasant, often overlooked circus film *Chad Hanna,* which starred Henry Fonda and Linda Darnell. And there are the elephants who provide a thunderous climax to *Elephant Walk,* a not-very-good Elizabeth Taylor film of life on a tea plantation.

Indeed, most jungle animals tend to serve merely as exotic background material for the movies. Even a film as good as *The African Queen* (1951), which had Humphrey Bogart and Katharine Hepburn at the top of their form, benefited from some fascinating shots of African wildlife. A less fascinating movie such as *Mogambo* (1953), which had Clark Gable, Ava Gardner, and Grace Kelly in an African triangle, is pepped up considerably by realistic animal footage (*Mogambo* had some truly impressive scenes of jungle gorillas). In the old days, directors would either use stock footage—toward the end of the Tarzan series, the same elephant stampede seemed to show up in every film— or, if the budget was big enough, would send a second unit to Africa to film wildlife; the actors would be worked into the animal footage by special-effects techniques back in the studio.

More recently, as the movie industry makes fewer

and more expensive films, the tendency has been to send everyone out on location to get the maximum in realism. Since wild animals are unpredictable and movie stars are expensive items, special techniques often are necessary even when the actors go on location. For example, in *King Solomon's Mines* (1950), the scene in which a rhinoceros walks across the path of Stewart Granger and Deborah Kerr was filmed with a number of armed hunters standing by, ready to shoot if the rhino should get violent (it didn't). The impressively realistic animal stampede scene in the film was made by first rounding up some animals and stampeding them for the benefit of the cameras and then filming the actors against that footage in the studio.

But the truth is that there's a limit to what filmmakers can do with really wild animals. Audiences do prefer the image of the wild animal who is really a gentle pet at heart, no matter how unrealistic that image might be. The demand for that sort of film is demonstrated constantly—in 1978, by Clint Eastwood, who costarred with an orangutan named Clyde in a comedy called *Every Which Way But Loose*. Clyde could smile bashfully, fling up his arms and fall down dead when someone said "bang," kiss human actors, and in general seem appealingly human. The critics found Clyde considerably more appealing than the rest of the movie.

The person who has benefited most from the image of the gentle wild animal probably is Ivan Tors,

Every Which Way But Loose
Clint Eastwood and Clyde the Orangutan. (Warners, 1978)

whose speciality is family entertainment. At the peak of his success, in the 1960s, Tors had dozens of African animals, from giraffes to lions, on a California ranch which he called Africa U.S.A. Tors was fond of explaining that the secret of his success was treating animals gently, rather than using the rough-and-tough techniques of other trainers. Among other films, Tors was responsible for *Clarence the Cross-Eyed Lion* (1965), which became the television series "Daktari"; *Gentle Giant* (1967), which became the television series "Gentle Ben"; and *Africa—Texas Style!* (1967), which became the television series "Cowboy in Africa." Tors's films generally featured lovable animals —although he was careful to say that he was "absolutely against any wild animals larger than an ocelot as pets." (But he did add that he might occasionally have a tiger over for a swim in his pool.)

However, Tors got his start with animals not on the African plains but underwater—a location which Hollywood has found to be quite profitable and one worth exploring.

Chapter Five

UNDERWATER ADVENTURES

As Ivan Tors told me, he was a successful screenwriter and film producer, who got started in a new career because he couldn't find a movie that was suitable for his six-year-old son, Steven, to see in Los Angeles. That same week, he was handed an outline for a film about a dolphin named Flipper. Tors went to Florida to work with the various dolphins who played Flipper and soon found himself being turned into an animal trainer.

Tors said he asked why all the people who trained dolphins stood out of the water. He found that the only reason was that the first man who ever trained a dolphin had been unable to swim, and everyone had been doing it the same way since. Tors then got into the tanks with the dolphins and found that the animals could pick up in three weeks tricks that had taken them six months to learn using the old method.

Flipper
A dolphin does a trick for his human friend, Luke Halpin.
(*MGM, 1970*)

"From that point I decided to throw away the book and learn animal training myself," he said.

Flipper was released in 1963 and was a box-office success; like many other Tors movies, it was turned into a television series. The dolphin was the most likely candidate for the first underwater animal star.

(As most people know, the dolphin, like the whale, is not a fish but a mammal who has adapted to life in the water. Unlike a fish, a dolphin or a whale can drown if held underwater too long.) Dolphins are known to be extremely intelligent animals. A dolphin's brain is not only larger than a human brain, but it is also larger in proportion to body size than the human brain. John Lilly, a scientist who has worked with dolphins for many years, has become convinced that dolphins actually are more intelligent than humans—intelligent enough to prevent humans from discovering what Lilly believes to be the secrets of the dolphin.

Dolphins are extremely powerful—they can jump twenty feet out of the water almost effortlessly—and are very easy to train. They are known to use a natural version of sonar in the water, emitting high-pitched tones so that objects can be located by detecting the echoes. Dolphins have been heard to emit a number of whistling, crackling, and buzzing sounds that some experts, notably Lilly, believe to be dolphin language. Dolphins can be excellent mimics. Mitzi, the three-hundred-pound female who did most of the work in *Flipper*, once heard a construction worker whistling a tune next to her tank. She immediately surfaced and whistled back, imitating his tone. Such incidents explain why Lilly believes that it might be possible someday to achieve vocal communication between dolphins and humans—although it must be added that the same techniques that have been used to teach words to chimpanzees have thus far failed when tried with dolphins.

To demonstrate what dolphins can do, Mitzi would respond to fifteen different hand signals, jumping high in the air, retrieving as many as five objects at once, shaking hands with her flipper, and snapping her tail in the water. She would tow a boat, using a rope with a noose—a skill she picked up in just a few hours—and would allow an actor to ride along underwater by holding onto a flipper. Since dolphins are air-breathing mammals, Mitzi could be transported easily from her home, the Miami Seaquarium, by taking her out of the water on a stretcher and putting her in a water-filled container. She was intelligent enough to recognize when a move was planned and to swim toward the net that would lift her out of the water.

Mitzi did seem to have that special quality that makes an animal into a star. When she died in 1971 of a heart attack, her owner said, "There wasn't another one like her in the world and there never will be. She was a ham from the word go. She loved people and she loved applause."

Both in the movies and on television, *Flipper* was a clean, happy show, in which everything always worked out for the best. The next dolphin movie to come along was a much more sinister matter. It was *The Day of the Dolphin* (1973), which was based loosely on Lilly's dolphin research and on apparently true reports that the Navy has trained dolphins to be used as living weapons.

The plot had George C. Scott as a Lilly-like scientist who finally succeeded in teaching a dolphin named Alpha to speak English (something that definitely has not happened in real life). At that point, mysterious things began to happen, and the plot thickens so rapidly that it almost coagulates. Eventually, the audience learned that the Establishment villains have plans to make living torpedoes out of the dolphins by strapping bombs to their backs. The critics loved the dolphins, liked the blue-water scenery, but thought that the movie itself was decidedly a loser.

Other than dolphins, the list of real-life underwater animals who have made it in the movies is very short. Perhaps the most interesting of these animals was a killer whale—not actually a whale at all, but the largest member of the dolphin family—who blundered into a fisherman's net off the coast of British Columbia in 1965. An entrepreneur named Ted Griffin brought the killer whale, which was given the name of Namu, to the Seattle Marine Aquarium and managed to keep it alive for a prolonged period. It was quite an achievement. Few killer whales have been captured alive, and most of them have died quickly of infections. The animals are used to the relatively germ-free water of the open sea and are vulnerable to the polluted water of harbors.

It wasn't long before Ivan Tors appeared and began making a film that was called *Namu the Killer Whale*, which was based pretty much on the facts in the case, and won the usual favorable reviews as "good family fare." The movie was released in 1966, and it was the only one Namu ever made. In July of that year, Namu died, ironically enough, by drowning, in an apparent effort to escape from its waterfront pen. Namu made a rush toward the nets between it and the open ocean, became entangled, and drowned before he could be released. Loneliness could have been listed as the cause of death. It was the mating season, and Namu was responding to an instinctive urge to join his own kind when he tried to crash through to freedom.

The next underwater animal to make a big splash in the movies was to become the most famous—and most menacing—of all: the shark in *Jaws* (1976), which scared so many people so quickly that it became the second biggest box-office attraction in film history up to that time. However, an asterisk has to be put next to this entry, because the shark in *Jaws* was not a real animal at all. Unlike dolphins, sharks are not very intelligent animals, and they are quite dangerous to work with. Therefore, the shark in *Jaws*—the film crew nicknamed it Bruce—was really three different models of a Great White shark. Two of the models were mechanized, one showing the shark's left profile and the other, the right profile. The third was a model of a whole shark that floated and that could be towed by a motorboat for high-speed swimming. Each of the models had skin made of polyurethane, coated with sand for realism, and each had two sets of teeth, one hard and one soft, which could be changed for different scenes. The models were so loaded with valves and controls that Bruce weighed forty-two tons, compared to about two tons for a real Great White shark.

Jaws
Bruce the shark does his mechanized bit. (Universal, 1976)

In *Jaws*, the shark that terrorized a Long Island town came to a bad end when it was blown up at the climax of the film. In real life, Bruce was simply dumped on a back lot at Universal Studios, where the models quietly rotted away. When the time came to make *Jaws 2*, it took two years and more than two million dollars to rehabilitate the models. They got new skin, new teeth, and what amounted to a facelift. For the first film, the shark's jaws were designed to stay open, which gave them a jowly look. The chin flab was removed for *Jaws 2*. Bruce was also given some new talents, including the ability to make complete turns and roll his eyes, all of which added some thirteen tons to the model's weight.

Although the shark's performance in *Jaws 2* was impressively realistic, the sequel did not match the box-office performance of *Jaws*. But *Jaws* did start a whole new trend in animal movies, as producers began to see possibilities in films about killer animals. Until then, setting aside such stereotypes as the wicked wolf, the big-earning movie animals had all been heroes. Now a rash of films which had animals as villains appeared. Dino de Laurentiis led the charge with a movie featuring a killer whale, which, unlike Namu, was really a killer. The film was *Orca* (1977), whose plot had Richard Harris as a fisherman who hoped to make money by capturing a killer whale but who killed a pregnant female whale. From then on, the bereaved male mate stalked the fisherman. There was an ample supply of seagoing violence before the finale, but not enough of a plot to impress either critics or audiences. One critic called *Orca* "a spaghetti sea saga"; another described it as "total immersion in the ridiculous," and the film sank without a trace.

Another attempt to capitalize on the *Jaws* phenomenon was *Greed* (1978), which featured a Brazilian lake that contained both a hoard of stolen jewels and an ample supply of piranhas, the ferocious, razor-teethed tropical killer fish. The movie was notable mostly for the difficulties that were encountered when the filmmakers worked with the piranhas. The first batch of piranhas, captured in a tributary of the Amazon River, ate through the plastic containers in which they were stored while they were being flown to the Atlantic Coast location where the movie was being made. The second batch of piranhas was transported in glass containers, made it successfully to the set—and proceeded to devour each other mercilessly as soon as they were put into a tank for preliminary filming.

A fish expert was called in and quickly diagnosed the problem. Piranhas are among the most ferocious animals on earth, in the water or out; they have been reported to eat large animals such as horses down to the bones in a matter of minutes. On the movie set, the irritable piranhas would sense that one of their own was weak and tired and would turn on it. That would arouse a killer instinct that nothing could stop until the piranhas had literally devoured one another. The fish expert would stand alongside the piranha pool looking for tired fish. When he spotted one, he would pull it out of the water and massage it back into shape. Those measures kept the piranhas alive to film the two key scenes, in one of which they made a quick, bloody meal of the character played by Lee Majors of Six Million Dollar Man fame.

The piranha difficulties illustrate why fish and other underwater animals have rarely achieved film stardom. They just aren't easy to handle. And, with the exception of dolphins, they are not creatures with whom humans identify. As a result, seagoing creatures almost always appear in movies as menaces. The octopus, a shy, retiring creature whose habits are fascinating to marine biologists, shows up in films only as a threat to divers; invariably, the octopus is the attacker. What devoted moviegoer cannot remember numberless repetitions of the scene in which a slimy tentacle makes a slow, threatening appearance at the corner of the screen. We know that the hero will soon be in a struggle for life, slashing at tentacles in a cloud of ink.

Possibly the greatest of those unrealistic scenes was in a 1942 Cecil B. De Mille epic, *Reap the Wild Wind*, which had John Wayne fighting a giant squid (a close relative of the octopus) during a nineteenth-century dive off Georgia. On a different scale, there have been equally impressive scenes featuring giant squids or octopuses. In *20,000 Leagues Under the Sea* (a 1954 Walt Disney version of the Jules Verne novel), Captain Nemo's submarine, *Nautilus*, is attacked by a giant squid which was created by the special-effects department: a full-sized model that required sixteen men to operate it. In *It Came from Beneath the Sea,* special-effects expert Ray Harryhausen created the giant octopus that oozed from the depths to attack San Francisco.

It can readily be seen that the line between real animals and creatures of the imagination is somewhat nebulous in the movies. Namu the killer whale was a real animal. But when John Huston made his 1956 film version of Herman Melville's classic whaling novel, *Moby Dick,* it was necessary to use a model for the whale—a ninety-foot, thirty-ton, electrically powered sperm whale that could dive, spout water, and otherwise comport itself as a real whale would. (The model was, however, not nearly as seaworthy as a real whale. The first two models broke loose during bad weather and disappeared. It was a third model that was used for the climactic scene in which Moby Dick sinks the whaling vessel, the *Pequod,* and claims its obsessed master, Captain Ahab, who is last seen entangled in harpoons and ropes on the side of Moby Dick, beckoning the *Pequod* on to its doom.)

As Hollywood has found, the line between filming a real whale and a model of a whale, or a real squid and a model of a giant squid, is easy to cross. What is more, crossing that line has proved to be profitable. Some of Hollywood's greatest animal film stars have never existed anywhere but on film.

Chapter Six

BIGGER THAN LIFE

You can get a real debate started by asking which are the biggest stars: the real animals that have dominated the movie screen or the make-believe animals that have been invented through the genius of Hollywood's special-effects departments and animation artists?

On the one hand you have such unquestioned stars as Rin Tin Tin, Lassie, and Trigger. On the other hand you have a truly impressive roster of animals who never existed but who have come to occupy a major position in modern folklore, not only in the United States but also in every country where films are shown: King Kong, Godzilla, Mickey Mouse, Donald Duck, and others.

(The idea has fictional possibilities. In the 1930s, James Thurber wrote a short story about a man who, saying jokingly that Donald Duck was a better actor than his wife's choice, Greta Garbo, began to defend the idea seriously and broke up his marriage in the process.)

The powerful hold of imaginary film animals on the American consciousness was demonstrated vividly in 1978, when the fiftieth anniversary of Mickey Mouse was celebrated. The events included a White House appearance in which the President's daughter, Amy Carter, met with Mickey; a ninety-minute television special; a cross-country whistle-stop train tour featuring an actor dressed in a Mickey Mouse costume; installation of a plaque in the Broadway threater where the first Mickey Mouse short was shown; an exhibition of Mickey Mouse memorabilia in the Library of Congress; and a month-long Mickey Mouse retrospective at the prestigious Museum of Modern Art in New York. All these marks of respect for Mickey by the Establishment were accompanied by a brisk sale of Mickey Mouse merchandise, from the familiar wristwatches to drinking glasses, place mats, and posters. And all of this for a character whose last film was made in 1953, long before today's child fans were born.

Beginnings are everything. Mickey Mouse was born during a long, despondent train ride that Walt Disney took from New York to California early in 1928. Disney had been making a series of cartoons about a character called Oswald the Rabbit, and he had been told in New York that Oswald had been wrested away from him in a corporate power play by his partners.

You can't keep a good mouse down; some of the latest versions of the classic Mickey Mouse watch.

In a magazine article issued many years later over his name, Walt Disney told a romantic story of how the idea of another cartoon animal began to emerge from his thoughts, and of how the concept finally arrived of making the animal "a romping, rollicking little mouse." According to the article, even the train whistle screeched, "A m-m-owause." By the time the train was in the Middle West, the article went on, Disney had decided to dress the mouse in a pair of red velvet pants with two pearl buttons.

Disney first named the character Mortimer Mouse, but quickly changed the first name to Mickey. The character that appeared in the first Mickey Mouse film short to be screened, *Steamboat Willie,* was designed to be simple, because Disney's studio had to push out a lot of film in a hurry. The head was a circle, the nose was an oblong circle, the ears were two big circles, the body was pear-shaped, the arms and legs were lines, and the feet were boxlike.

Mickey had one huge break: he appeared just at the time when the screen had discovered sound. In fact, *Steamboat Willie,* in which Mickey made his screen debut, was the third Mickey Mouse cartoon that Disney made, but the first to have sound—an ingenious musical sound track that was written to accentuate the animals gags in the film. The first two cartoons, *Plane Crazy* and *Gallopin' Gaucho,* had no takers until they, too, were given sound tracks after the success of *Steamboat Willie.*

Learned volumes have been written in an effort to

explain why Mickey Mouse should be so successful. Such an august figure as the great psychiatrist, Carl Jung, once explained ponderously that the secret was Mickey's circular shape—because, as Jung went on, the simple circle portrays "the archetype of self which, as we know from experience, plays the chief role in uniting apparently irreconcilable opposites and is therefore best suited to compensate the split-mindedness of the age."

Walt Disney, who made no claims of being a profound philosopher, had his own explanation, "All we ever intended for him or expected of him was that he should continue to make people everywhere chuckle with him and at him," Disney once said. "We didn't burden him with any social symbolism; we made him no mouthpiece for frustrations or harsh satire. Mickey was simply a little personality assigned to the purposes of laughter."

Whatever the answer, Mickey Mouse was a success at every level. Arturo Toscanini saw a Mickey Mouse cartoon, *The Band Concert,* in 1935, and asked for it to be rerun because the great conductor enjoyed Mickey's parody of Toscanini's behavior on the podium. That same year, the New York *Times* reported that "the King of England won't go to the movies unless Mickey Mouse is on the bill." President Roosevelt showed Mickey Mouse cartoons in the White House. And the public so loved not only Mickey Mouse cartoons but also Mickey Mouse merchandise so well that Mickey is credited with saving three companies during the dark days of the Depression—not only Walt Disney's studio (which was transformed from a small, struggling outfit to a Hollywood power), but also Lionel Trains, which made a killing turning out model handcars carrying Mickey and his girl friend, Minnie, and Ingersoll Watches, which brought out the Mickey Mouse wristwatch in 1933 and, after only eight weeks, had to hire 2,700 more employees to meet the demand.

(In passing, the Mickey Mouse wristwatch itself deserves a history. Among other indications of its incredible appeal are reports that Soviet soldiers spent as much as $1,000 for a Mickey Mouse watch in bartering with American troops in 1945. And when Emperor Hirohito of Japan visited Disneyland in 1975, he was openly pleased to be given a Micky Mouse watch as a memento of the trip.)

Over the years, Mickey's appearance changed as the animators tinkered with their drawings. He became rounder, smoother, more suave. His character also changed. Originally, Mickey was a troublemaker. As the Disney studio developed more cartoon animal characters, Mickey became a straight man, setting up gags for Goofy, the clumsy dog, and for irascible Donald Duck. Mickey now was the good guy who had a romantic interest, Minnie Mouse, who was bedecked with a bow, high heels, and lace-edged panties.

The hallmark of Disney cartoons during the peak years of Mickey Mouse and his gang was a painstaking dedication to quality. Disney is credited with setting new standards for color fidelity on film. His cartoonists were an elite group, handpicked from a mob of applicants and put through training that lasted for years. Careful attention was paid to every last detail, with both music and speech being synchronized to the characters' movements. Technically, the Disney shorts, lasting only seven to eight minutes, usually were far ahead of the main features on the same bill.

In all, 118 Mickey Mouse cartoons were released between 1928 and 1952. The changing nature of the entertainment business was blamed for bringing the series to an end. The cartoons were made primarily to be shown as part of an evening-long double feature. When television arrived, the double feature faded out and so did cartoon shorts. One other factor was involved. Cartoon shorts never were really big moneymakers, and the Disney studio (the Mouse House, as insiders called it) was devoting most of its effort to full-length cartoon features, such as *Snow White and the Seven Dwarfs*.

Before the series ended, Mickey Mouse had lost a lot of the favor he enjoyed with the critics. There were learned articles complaining that Mickey's world had become too goody-goody, and that Mickey's gang had been robbed of their sharpness by prosperity, respectability, and complacency. As Mickey's star fell in critical esteem, more reviewers began saying that first place had been taken over by a much more abrasive character, the star of Warner Brothers Looney Tunes and Merrie Melodies: Bugs Bunny.

What's up, doc? Mel Blanc, the voice of Bugs Bunny, wearing a sweater with a modern picture of the famous rabbit.

Bugs Bunny certainly was no goody-goody. With a tough Brooklyn accent (provided by Mel Blanc, who also provided the voices for all the other cartoon characters in the Warners stable), Bugs spent his time in never-ending conflict with enemies such as Elmer Fudd, whose only fault was to have intruded on Bugs's turf. While everything was jolly in the world of Mickey Mouse, the world of Bugs Bunny featured what amounted to straight violence—all done for fun and all beautifully choreographed, but violence nonetheless. Bugs Bunny's only redeeming quality was that he was almost unfailingly funny. Bugs respected no person, however dignified, and no institution, no matter how elevated.

A large part of Bugs Bunny's success was due to Mel Blanc and his amazingly versatile voice. Blanc broke in with what was then Leon Schlesinger Studios in 1937 (the organization later became the Warners cartoon studio). It began, Blanc later recalled, when he was asked, "Can you do a drunken bull?" He could and did.

Next came the voice of Porky Pig, which Blanc said was more an oink than a stammer—"like a pig actually would talk." Bugs Bunny made his first appearance in a 1940 cartoon called *The Happy Hare,* and Blanc said he provided Bugs with the toughest accent he could provide—mostly Brooklyn, but with a mixture of the Bronx.

There are differing stories of how Bugs got his celebrated tag line, "What's up, doc?" Some said that the line came from a young animator, who used to go around the studio saying, "What's up, doc?" so often that they finally wrote it into the script. But Blanc maintained that the studio originally wanted Bugs to say, "Hey, what's cookin'," but the phrase didn't sound modern enough for an up-to-date rabbit like Bugs. "At the time, 'What's up, doc?' was a very popular expression, so I suggested that Bugs use it," Blanc recalled.

Another one of Bugs's trademarks, his penchant for munching on carrots, caused Blanc no end of trouble. The story is that Bob Clampett, who created Bugs, saw a scene in the classic comedy, *It Happened One Night,* which had Clark Gable chewing a raw carrot. Just the habit for a rabbit, Clampett said. Unfortunately, the indispensable Mel Blanc was allergic to carrots, and the only way to catch the sound of Bugs munching on a carrot was to have Mel Blanc munch. (The munching was part of the dialogue, so no one else could do it.) The studio tried everything else it could think of, from turnips to celery, but nothing sounded like a carrot but the real thing. So all through the years, Mel Blanc would chomp a carrot and then quickly spit it out—something that might have helped Bugs achieve his nastier tones.

In the movies, Mel Blanc provided almost all the voices for some three thousand cartoons. He also created some imaginary animals for the Jack Benny radio show—first the growl of Carmichael the bear, who guarded Benny's underground vaults, and then the sarcastic voice of the parrot who was always sassing Benny by calling him "cheapskate!" In all, Mel Blanc created voices for some four hundred characters —including the ancient Maxwell automobile that coughed and died on Benny's radio show.

(The Walt Disney organization, on the other hand, used many different sources for its cartoon animals' voices. Walt Disney himself provided the voice of Mickey Mouse until 1946, when Walt became too busy to do it and the job was taken over by Jim Mac-Donald, a studio sound-effects man. The voice of Donald Duck was provided by Clarence Nash, who was making a living doing bird and animal imitations when Disney discovered him.)

Cartoon animals proliferated through the 1940s. There were Sylvester the Cat and Tweety Pie the Canary (whose line was, "I taut I taw a puddy tat"), Tom and Jerry (Tom was the cat and Jerry was the mouse), and many others. The animators who worked in those days agree on two things today. Walt Disney is given the credit for establishing the animated cartoon, not only because Disney created the very concept of a cartoon animal with a real personality but also because he—aided chiefly by a genius named Ub Iwerks, who has little fame outside the business but is renowned by insiders—set new technical standards for cartoons.

Those standards now are lost. When old-time animators reminisce, they dwell wonderingly on the quality of the work they used to do, as compared to what they regard as the cheap, slipshod work that goes into today's television cartoons. Numbers can tell much of the story. For a single six-minute cartoon of the 1930s or 1940s, animators would draw about six thousand cartoons. Today, only three thousand drawings go into a typical half-hour television cartoon. And while only animators may notice the loss of detail, anyone who has seen a recent animated cartoon can testify that the new ones just aren't as funny as the ones of the classic era. Worst of all, the craftsmanship which made the great animal cartoon characters come to life is dying out, because the current crop of animators aren't getting anything like the training that once was mandatory.

Is it mere nostalgia that makes movie fans think that the imaginary animals of the past were better? Posing that question invites the same endless debate you can start by asking whether the baseball players of yesteryear were better than today's high-priced stars. But it is certain that one film animal of the past has established a position that is virtually unchallenged.

That animal is King Kong—and one hastens to add that it is the original King Kong of the 1933 film. Like the original Mickey Mouse films, *King Kong* established a new standard for the movies—in this case, a standard for special effects. In the decades to follow, others were to improve upon some of the techniques used in *King Kong,* but those techniques were the starting point for virtually every effort in the field.

While King Kong is too menacing a creature to be

King Kong
The one and only scares the wits out of actress Fay Wray in the classic film. (RKO, 1933)

idolized in the way that Mickey Mouse is, the image of the giant gorilla who dies for love is so fascinating that a solid shelf of books and an apparently endless stream of articles have been written about Kong—everything from detailed technical descriptions of the special-effects techniques used to create Kong to learned treatises saying that the King Kong story is actually an allegory of the way in which Europe has oppressed the Third World.

The story of the giant ape, who is worshiped as a god on a mysterious island, is captured by an ambitious filmmaker, breaks free to terrorize a city and kidnap the girl with whom the ape apparently has fallen in love, and finally is shot down by airplanes from the top of the Empire State Building, was produced and directed by Merian C. Cooper, using methods developed by Willis H. O'Brien.

O'Brien was the pioneer in the use of models to create realistic-looking but imaginary creatures. The original King Kong, for example, never existed in full size. Most of the film was made by using eighteen-inch-high models with ball-and-socket joints. O'Brien would shoot one frame of film, move the model a fraction of an inch, shoot another frame, and so on until the picture of a real, moving ape was achieved. Days were needed to get only a few feet of film, and more time was needed for the special techniques by which the actors were included in the action. Years later, Cooper told a magazine how one scene, in which King Kong picked at the clothing of actress Fay Wray, was made: "A movie was first taken of her alone while invisible wires pulled off her clothes. Then the miniature Kong was placed on a set built on a waist-high platform, about twice the size of a dining-room table, on which miniature trees, ferns, and plaster-of-Paris rocks had been arranged. Back of this, the movie of Fay

Wray was projected and Kong's movements made to correspond with it."

Parts of Kong were built for special scenes. A giant hand was built for the shots in which King Kong grabbed Fay Wray and carried her away. And a model of Kong's head and shoulders, twenty feet high, was built for close-ups, including the frightening scene in which Kong's face suddenly appears outside Fay Wray's hotel room. But otherwise, "the eighth wonder of the world," as Kong was introduced in the film, was no more than a handful of models covered with rabbit fur.

Still, Cooper had created a new kind of film character: an outsized ape with personality. Unhappily, later attempts to create similar characters fell short of the original. The star of the inevitable sequel, *Son of Kong*, also released in 1933, was an albino who was a lot shorter than his father and who generated a lot less interest. *Mighty Joe Young* (1949) was a good-guy, tame giant ape who was goaded into violence but who emerged a hero by saving some children from an orphanage fire. The special effects, done this time by another master, Ray Harryhausen, were impressive, but Joe was no real challenge to the original King.

And despite all the hullabaloo about an expensive and well-publicized 1976 remake of the original plot, the new *King Kong* did nothing to erase memories of the old Kong. The 1976 film was made by Dino de Laurentiis, who boasted that it had a $25-million

King Kong
The modern version, with the giant ape after his fall from the World Trade Center. The actress is Jessica Lange. (Paramount, 1976)

budget. This time there was at least one full-scale model of Kong. It was used for the last scene of the film, in which the ape has fallen to his death. The new movie substituted the twin towers of the World Trade Center for the Empire State Building and had the shooting done by army helicopters rather than by the biplanes of the old movie. An open invitation was issued for New Yorkers to provide the crowd for the final scene, and 25,000 of them turned out to gasp at the model of Kong's crumpled body on the pavement.

It was all great publicity. And the reviewers agreed that the special effects (credited to Carlo Rambaldi, Glen Robinson, and Rick Baker) were quite impressive. But the general feeling was that one King Kong was enough, and that the first one was preferable to the new, improved model. The 1976 movie was reported to be a financial success, but it had nothing like the psychological impact of the original. It seemed to come and go in a flash, while revivals of the first *King Kong* continued to flourish.

However, a rival for Kong did emerge, in an unexpected form and from an unanticipated source. In 1964, the Japanese studio Toho made a monster movie about a giant lizard who is awakened from his prehistoric sleep by an American nuclear bomb test off the coast of Japan. In the film, the monster destroys some ships by simply breathing on them, then comes ashore to level much of Tokyo. The lizard eventually is stopped by a secret weapon called the "oxygen destroyer," developed by a Japanese scientist.

The film was a hit in Asian cities, and Toho decided to try it in the American market. They hired Raymond Burr (in the days before he achieved wealth and fame as television's Perry Mason), spent a day shooting scenes of him as an American reporter named Steve Martin who covers the monster story,

Godzilla
The monster goes wild in Tokyo. (Toho, 1956)

changed the name of the film from *Gojira* to *Godzilla, King of the Monsters,* and released the film in the United States in 1956. It hit the jackpot. Indeed, *Godzilla* was the first Japanese movie ever to succeed outside the art-house circuit in America. (It was helped by the fact that Raymond Burr's name was displayed prominently above the title, leading a lot of moviegoers to believe that the movie they were about to see wasn't Japanese at all.)

Came the sequels. The first one was called either *Godzilla Raids Again* or *Gigantis the Fire Monster,* depending on which theater you happened to see it in. The next one was *Godzilla vs. Mothra* (1961), in which the big lizard underwent a drastic change in character. Instead of being a villain, Godzilla now was the hero who saved Japan from Mothra, a giant caterpillar who devoured everything in sight. By 1979, a total of seventeen Godzilla films had been made, and he was the good guy in all but the first two. The critics greeted all the Godzilla films with a sort of amused disdain, but the big lizard had managed to capture the hearts and minds of people who paid for their tickets.

Special-effects work was one of the major reasons for Godzilla's success. The Japanese used their own method. Rather than building small models of the animal, they used actors inside rubber suits and built scale models of the cities. The Tokyo through which Godzilla and the other monsters rampaged so often was actually an exquisitely designed miniature metropolis that covered two full city blocks. Another reason for the box-office appeal of Godzilla was the variety of his enemies. In various films, Godzilla has fought Ghidrah the Three-Headed Monster, something called the Smog Monster (which feeds on factory fumes and auto exhausts), a giant bird that created typhoons by flapping its wings and none other than King Kong. With tact, the Japanese filmed two endings to *King Kong vs. Godzilla* (1963). In the version that was shown in Japan, Godzilla beat King Kong to a pulp. But in the film that appeared in the United States, King Kong struggled to his feet and threw Godzilla out to sea, gaining victory by a TKO.

By the late 1970s, Godzilla films settled down to a comfortable formula. Toho was making two films a year. Each cost in the neighborhood of $1.2 million and could be counted on to earn about $20 million. Godzilla had become a world traveler. In *Godzilla vs. Amphibion,* he turned up in the Bermuda Triangle, while in *Godzilla vs. the Alien Invasion,* he emerged from Lake Michigan. There were Godzilla T-shirts, Godzilla jigsaw puzzles, Godzilla comic books, and even a Godzilla record. The Japanese had come up with many other monsters, including Rodan, a giant flying reptile, and Gammera, a flying turtle who could shoot fire, but Godzilla clearly was in a class by himself for audience appeal.

One question about the imaginary animals of the movies is where to draw the line. For example, should the apes in *Planet of the Apes* (1967), and the four

Chewbacca the Wookie helps Luke Skywalker and Han Solo, who are disguised as enemy soldiers. (20th Century-Fox, 1977)

sequels that it inspired, be included in the roster? And how about Chewbacca, the monkey-faced, furry, blue-eyed Wookie who was copilot on a spaceship with Han Solo (played by Harrison Ford) in the 1977 smash hit *Star Wars?* For that matter, how about all the strange creatures who congregated in the spaceport bar in one of the most imaginative scenes of *Star Wars?* Those creatures were almost literally indescribable, but they were supposed to be as intelligent as human beings. (Chewbacca did have the disconcerting habit, according to a half-joking remark in the film, of ripping the arm off anyone who beat him in a game of animated chess. But Chewbacca also had the intelligence to be a crew member on a spaceship, which is more than can be said for King Kong or Godzilla.)

Fortunately, it isn't necessary to draw the line too clearly. One of the enjoyable things about the movies is that they can erase many of the lines that exist in real life, so that audiences can enjoy blue-eyed Wookies and humanoid apes, giant lizards who come to the aid of mankind, and huge gorillas who fall in love with young girls, mice who wear velvet trousers and rabbits who talk with a Brooklyn accent. With imaginary animals, relax and enjoy.

Chapter Seven

ALL THE BEASTS
AND BIRDS

Question: If you were writing a book about movie animals, would you include Francis the Talking Mule in the chapter on horses?

In this book, the answer is "no," by a hairsbreadth. To start with, there is the fact that Francis, like all mules, is the offspring of a male donkey and a female horse, which makes it only half a horse by descent. To this must be added the ability to talk, which moves Francis closer to the imaginary-animal category. But on the other hand, one must weigh the fact that Francis was the inspiration for "Mr. Ed," a television show about a talking horse. The best way to decide the issue is to put Francis in the category of "miscellaneous animal," the subject of this chapter.

Anyway, the talking mule made its debut in a 1949 Universal film called *Francis,* which set the style for the six sequels that followed. The premise of all the films was that Francis, an Army mule, had more horse sense than its human sidekick, who was played through most of the series by Donald O'Connor. The plot was always the same: the O'Connor character (named Peter Stirling in the films) would get into hot water and Francis would not only get him out of trouble but would make him a hero to boot.

The Francis films featured some good actresses and actors. You could see Zasu Pitts and Tony Curtis in the first film, Piper Laurie and Cecil Kellaway in the sequel, *Francis Goes to the Races* (1951), and the likes of Martha Hyer, Mamie Van Doren, David Janssen, Jim Backus, and Clint Eastwood in other films of the series. For the final movie, *Francis in the Haunted House* (1956), Mickey Rooney replaced Donald O'Connor as Francis' human partner.

Throughout the series, the voice of Francis was the old Western character actor, the late Chill Wills (who also made an on-the-screen appearance as General "Mustard Ben" Kaye in *Francis Joins the Wacs,* released in 1954). Wills once explained his success in the films by saying, "I used to skin mules down in the Oklahoma oil fields. I learned their language. I had to beg them to take me home." Wills so identified with the down-to-earth personality of Francis that he often threw away the script and made up his own dialogue. The only film for which Wills did not supply Francis' voice was the last one, in which Paul Frees did the talking.

There was one amusing sidelight to the Francis

Francis Joins the Wacs
The mule poses with some starlets and his old friend, Donald O'Connor. (Universal, 1954)

series. It took a year after the success of the first film for Universal to decide on doing a sequel. While the executives talked, Francis was eating—eating so much that the mule got overweight. Jimmy Phillips, the mule's trainer, was ordered to take 250 pounds off Francis or lose the part. It took a combination of strict dieting and strenuous exercise to slim Francis down to the desired weight.

If a mule could become a film star, why not a bear? In the 1970s, a bear with star qualities did emerge as a major box-office attraction. Bozo the bear made her first appearance in a 1975 film called *The Life and Times of Grizzly Adams,* which was based on the nineteenth-century historical character named James Capen Adams. In real life, Adams does not seem to have been the most charming individual; after committing a crime, he fled to the Rocky Mountains in 1853 to avoid the law and, thereafter, lived in the wild. He got to know the ways of wild animals well enough to trap them alive and sell them to zoos and circuses. In the ecology-conscious 1970s, this character was transformed into a warm, tender human being who romped with porcupines, bobcats, raccoons, and all the other creatures of a wilderness that seemed rather suburban. Chief among those creatures was Bozo, who did have unusual characteristics for a bear.

While bears are not unusually ferocious if left alone, they are not animals with whom humans usually want to cavort. Bozo was different. She was found in a circus by Lloyd Beebe, an animal handler who lives in

The Life and Times of Grizzly Adams
Bozo the bear and Dan Haggerty in the film that led to their
television series. (Sunn, 1975)

the state of Washington. No one knew where Bozo came from, but it was clear that she was unusually gentle for a bear. In particular, there was a warm rapport between Bozo and an animal trainer named Dan Haggerty—who is something of a bear himself, standing six foot one inch tall and having the build of a football lineman. Haggerty could play with Bozo in a way that zoologists said would be impossible; the bear would literally lie down and roll over gently for Haggerty.

It was possible to argue with the logic behind the human-bear relationship in *The Life and Times of Grizzly Adams,* on the grounds that no real nineteenth-century frontiersman viewed a bear as anything other than a sworn enemy, rather than the warm friend of the movie character. But no one was going to argue with the economics of the film. It cost about $140,000 to produce and earned a whopping $65 million at the box office. Pausing only to make an equally successful not-quite sequel titled *The Adventures of Frontier Fremont,* the Grizzly Adams group was off to what turned out to be a remarkably successful television series.

Anyone who thinks that the warm relationships between animals and humans that were shown in the Grizzly Adams film were real should not put that thought into action. The truth is that the wild animals in the film had no warm feelings for humans at all. Bozo had four doubles—bear look-alikes—and every one of them had to be restrained by charged electric wires when they went through their paces. The other animals, such as the rabbits and the raccoons, were trained in the classic style, by giving them rewards in the form of food when they did their tricks. The animal would be taught to do a specific task—say, knocking over a pot—when a buzzer sounded, and would be given food as a reward for performing the task. Captured on film, the results looked remarkably spontaneous and heart-warming; they especially appealed to a city-bred generation who thought that life in the untamed wilderness might be fun. In real life, romping with bears and other wild animals is a prescription for some rather unpleasant experiences.

But it must be said that in its own peculiar way, Hollywood managed to make at least one film which made a villainous bear seem even more improbable than a friendly bear. The film was *Grizzly* (1976), which was distinguished chiefly as an imitation of *Jaws*. In *Grizzly,* the bear was an unadulterated villain who terrorized the campers in a national park, killing and maiming humans for no particular reason. The film was a dismal flop at the box office, which indicated either that audiences had a fairly realistic understanding of the way in which bears really live in the wild—they are quite peaceful citizens if they are untouched by humans—or that imitations of successful movies never do as well as the originals.

Either explanation is acceptable, because the thought patterns of movie audiences are difficult to interpret. To give one example, a film built around a

Willard
Bruce Davison feeds the army of trained rats that he will turn loose on his enemies. (Cinerama, 1971)

pack of murderous rats might not seem to be designed for audience appeal, but *Willard* (1971) was based on the premise and proved to be a hit. In outline, the plot does not appear to be the most attractive possible. It had Bruce Davison playing an ineffectual young man who one reviewer described as "the sort of fumbling, neurotic mess whom anonymous bus drivers delight in humiliating." This character, Willard, had just one ability: he could communicate with rats. For some reason, audiences took great pleasure in watching Willard turn his pack of pet rats loose on humans, including the rapacious businessman (played by Ernest Borgnine) who had taken away the company owned by Willard's father. In the end, Willard was consumed by the rats himself.

But the rats came back in *Ben* (1972), a sequel that was named, significantly, not after a human but after the chief rat of the pack that had been trained by Willard. *Ben* had a young man, played by Lee Harcourt Montgomery, adopting the rat pack after Willard was gnawed to death. Predictably, the rats in *Ben* created havoc in a health spa and a supermarket before the police, armed with flamethrowers and water hoses, wiped them out. Just in case there was a demand for another sequel, the producers had Ben the head rat survive. But two rat films were enough.

One movie with birds as the villains was enough, even though that film was made by the master of film suspense, Alfred Hitchcock. In 1963, Hitchcock made a film, *The Birds*, which was based on a story by

Daphne du Maurier. Even for such a master of the mysterious as Hitchcock, *The Birds* was an eerie film. It started with the heroine, Tippi Hedren, having an unfriendly encounter with a man in a bird shop. For no apparent reason, the girl is attacked by sea gulls, and then by a swarm of sparrows who swoop down a chimney into a living room. Unaccountably, the birds have gone mad, killing all humans whom they can attack with bill and claw. *The Birds* is especially chilling because the film never does provide an explanation for the violent behavior of the birds. The movie ends on a disturbingly inconclusive note, with the birds watching as the human stars edge toward safety.

For the filmmakers, the birds were a menace of a different sort. Birds are not at all easy to train—which explains why the roster of bird stars is rather short. There was an eagle named Old Admiral, trained by an animal handler named Curly Twilford, who appeared on the screen in the 1950s; and a raven named Jimmy, another Twilford protégé, who also made a number of screen appearances, but that's about it. Some three thousand birds were used for the Hitchcock film, but there was very little training involved. Either the birds were dumped on the actors in bulk or else the moviemakers used special-effects techniques, such as photographic process shots. The birds and the humans may have appeared to have been in the same scene, but most of the time they were really on two different rolls of film that were melded together by movie technicians. When contact between birds and actors was unavoidable, it invariably ended with the actors stalking away from the set, wiping themselves off and muttering curses.

That was pretty much the story for a 1962 film, *Birdman of Alcatraz,* in which the birds were supposed to be sympathetic characters. The film was based on the true story of a convict, Robert Stroud, who was sentenced to life in prison and who became one of the world's leading authorities on bird behavior through his patient work with caged birds in his cell. *Birdman of Alcatraz* featured many scenes in which the hero, played by Burt Lancaster, demonstrated his warm understanding of bird behavior. In fact, those scenes were made only with agonizingly difficult effort. The birds were trained by an expert, Ray Berwick, but director John Frankenheimer later recalled that the bright lights needed to film the scenes would petrify the birds. A lot of time was spent in waiting for the birds to perform their tasks. The waiting was especially painful, Frankenheimer said, because the entire set had to be enclosed in wire mesh so that the birds would not escape, which meant that everyone involved in making the movie became increasingly claustrophobic as filming went on.

That sort of difficulty explains why so few birds have become screen stars. It is harder to explain why there has been no star representative of an animal who might seem to be a natural: the cat. If dogs and horses can make it, then why have there been no feline counterparts of Rin Tin Tin and Trigger?

The answer to that question hinges on the personality of the cat and its relationship with humans. Even cat lovers acknowledge that their pets are independent types who do not rely as utterly on human help as do dogs and horses. In practical terms, this characteristic means that cats are not as ready to perform for the camera as dogs are. The most successful screen animals, those with true star quality, seem to like acting for its own sake. They do not reject the food and other awards they get, but they appear to enjoy what they do. However, as Frank Inn, a celebrated cat trainer for the movies, once explained, cats are in the business strictly for what they can get out of it. The best cat actors are gluttons, Inn said, because the hungriest cats perform most eagerly so they can get their tidbits. And the food had better be there for consumption as soon as a trick is over: no food, no more acting.

Still, there have been a number of movies which had cats in starring roles—although no cat has ever achieved the kind of continuing screen success that Lassie, Rin Tin Tin, and Benji did. Take the 1951 film *Rhubarb,* made from an H. Allen Smith novel, which had a cat inheriting the Brooklyn Dodgers (yes, the Dodgers were still in Brooklyn in those days) from an eccentric millionaire. Rhubarb was played by an ordinary alley cat, named Orangey, who was supplied by Frank Inn. Orangey was a mean cuss—exactly what the plot called for, which is why he got the role —but a few tricks could make him show affection.

When the script called for Rhubarb to lick the hand of his costar, Ray Milland, that was easy. Inn rubbed liver paste on Milland's hand, and Orangey licked it up.

But then Orangey lost his taste for liver. Inn quickly substituted catnip, which was applied to Milland's back or leg when the script called for Rhubarb to rub up against his master. And even with all these tricks, Orangey would not relax his stubborn ways enough to be usable in all the scenes of the film. Inn had to supply a total of twenty-two doubles to get the movie done.

Orangey nevertheless had enough star quality to make a career for himself in films. He played opposite Jackie Gleason in *Gigot* (1962), a comedy set in Paris, and he was Audrey Hepburn's cat in another comedy, *Breakfast at Tiffany's* (1961). Orangey even won a Patsy, the animal equivalent of an Oscar, for that role, but no one outside the film business noticed.

In recent years, the Disney organization has been responsible for most of the cats on the screen. One standard formula for clean family entertainment is to follow the adventures of a lovable or unusual animal, and the Disney folks have that formula down perfectly. *The Three Lives of Thomasina* (1963), *That Darn Cat!* (1965) and, more recently, *The Cat from Outer Space* (1968) are smooth examples of how such a movie should be made. *The Cat from Outer Space* starred a fifteen-month-old Abyssinian named Jake (with his sister, Amber, serving as double when needed), who played an extraterrestrial visitor named Zunar J5/90 Doric Fourseven. The plot had the space cat's spacecraft making a crash landing on earth, and had Jake facing the tough choice of leaving for home or staying to rescue a white Persian cat named Lucy Belle, the love interest in the film. Naturally, he stayed. And with the help of a magic collar that could make people levitate, he brought about a happy ending.

But when most people think about cats, happy endings are not inevitable. After all, cats are linked in folklore to witches and the devil, and that link shows up in the movies. In the 1934 film *The Black Cat,* Boris Karloff was a devil worshiper—something that didn't do much for the public image of your average cat. In a 1941 film with the same title but a different plot, a black cat was transformed magically into actress Gale Sondergaard. And in *Bell, Book and Candle,* a 1958 film about witchcraft in modern Manhattan, a cat named Pywacket served as the familiar of a bewitching witch who was played by Kim Novak. (A familiar is the animal sidekick of a witch or a warlock.)

Even a gentle Thomasina or a magic space cat cannot overcome that bad image, an image which is peculiar to cats in films. Dogs are good guys; horses are invariably friendly; even bears can be made to seem lovable; but somehow cats of all sizes induce chills. For every civilized Elsa the lioness, there have been a dozen killer lions who have gone after Tarzan with blood in their eyes. Cougars and jaguars are always good for a frightening sequence; tigers are invariably man-eaters.

Of course, cat lovers can always comfort themselves with the thought that other animals have even worse images. Take insects—and, yes, insects definitely are in the animal kingdom. Aside from Jiminy Cricket, the animated character in Walt Disney's version of *Pinocchio*, it is difficult to think of an insect who has played a friendly role. Any time an insect makes an appearance, it can be counted upon to threaten someone.

For a real scare, nothing will beat hordes of insects, as in *The Naked Jungle* (1954), which had Charlton Heston fighting off an invasion by an army of red ants who threatened his tropical plantation, or *Brigham Young* (1940), which had a swarm of locusts threatening the new Mormon settlements in Utah, only to be defeated by an attacking flock of sea gulls (an event that actually happened). In a real pinch, the moviemaker can introduce the menacing figure of a giant insect. Possibly the best film of that type was *Them* (1954), which had James Whitmore, Edmund Gwenn, and Joan Weldon tracking down and destroying a nest of giant ants, mutations produced by the radiation from early atomic tests.

From the filmmaker's point of view, insects are wonderful enemies. Audiences might shudder at the thought of wiping out lions or tigers or wolves, but no one will complain if giant ants are attacked with flamethrowers, grenades, and machine guns, as they were in *Them.* After all, people don't identify with the giant ants' point of view. The drawback in the giant-insect plot is that such creatures cannot exist. A giant insect is impossible for two reasons: insects get their oxygen not by breathing but by diffusion through their bodies, which is fine for tiny creatures but not for large animals; and insects rely on their rigid shells for support—again, something that works well on a small scale but is not possible above a certain size. A giant insect would literally squash itself, collapsing of its own weight. (For that matter, a gorilla as large as King Kong is an impossibility; its bones would not be able to support the weight of its body.)

But talk of giant insects is leading us away from the subject. A giant insect is an imaginary animal, which falls into a different category than the one we are discussing. It is time to turn to another subject, animals on television.

Chapter Eight

THE TELEVISION CROWD

One of the most penetrating comments that can be made about television is the observation that the two most famous animals who were products of the TV business made it not as actors but as personalities. One was a chimpanzee who appeared primarily on television talk shows, and the other was a cat who did nothing but pet-food commercials.

It is true that television has had a number of other animal stars, but almost all of them began in the movies before starting their TV careers. Rin Tin Tin, we have already noted, had been a Hollywood star for many years before starring in a television series. The same is true of Lassie. Gentle Ben, the bear, did much more work on television than in motion pictures, but the idea for the television series did come from the movie *The Life and Times of Grizzly Adams*. Flipper also made a movie premiere before beginning a career as the lovable friend of two clean, wholesome boys on a typical, if damp, television family show.

Television fans might bring up the name of an animal who apparently is an exception to the rule—Mr. Ed, the talking horse. At first glance, Mr. Ed appears to belong solely to the television screen, since he never made a movie. But a closer inspection shows that Mr. Ed was merely a thinly disguised version of Francis, the talking mule of film fame.

The last Francis film was made in 1956. As stated previously, the formula was wearing thin. Donald O'Connor had withdrawn from his role as Francis' foil, and Chill Wills did not provide the mule's voice in the final Francis epic. Arthur Lubin, who had directed six of the Francis films—all but the last one —then created Mr. Ed. The line of succession was so obvious that no one could fail to follow it.

There were some differences. Instead of a mule, the talking animal was a handsome palomino horse. And instead of Donald O'Connor, the talking animal's human friend was played by Alan Young, an English-born comedian. But the essential situation was the same: the horse was smarter than his master; the master kept getting in trouble because people thought him peculiar when he talked to the horse; and the animal always got the human out of trouble when the episode ended.

"Mr. Ed," the television show, is interesting because it broke one of the most basic rules in TV programming. For economic reasons, television series almost

Mr. Ed
Alan Young and the talking horse of television fame.

invariably begin as network productions. A television episode costs so much to produce that only a network can afford to finance it. In many cases, the producer does not make a profit on the first showing of a TV series episode. The real profits are made after a series ends its network life. The series then goes into syndication—that is, the whole package is peddled to non-network stations, who can show the old episodes over and over again. The most popular television series, such as "I Love Lucy," may go on literally for decades in syndication after their network showings end.

"Mr. Ed" was one of the very few television series to do it the other way around. "Mr. Ed" began as a low-budget syndicated series. It proved to be such a hit on local stations that the CBS television network picked up the show after three years. "Mr. Ed" then went on to have a long run on the network before it went the way of all television series.

Alan Young later explained that he kept turning down Arthur Lubin's offer to do the television series, because of that understandable reluctance that any actor has to costarring with an animal. But after Young agreed to take on the series, he developed a liking for Mr. Ed, who began his acting career in the series. Young once told an interviewer that Mr. Ed "is a real ham"—a statement that indicates some degree of respect for a fellow actor. According to Young, Mr. Ed enjoyed the public exposure he got when he was driven to the studio along the freeways of Los Angeles. "He looks out as though he's saying, 'This is my public,' and nods to people. When he comes out of the trailer at the studio with his tail flying out behind him, we all know it will be a good day. If his tail is tucked in, he doesn't feel like working. He works for obedience rather than rewards."

. That remark indicates that Mr. Ed did have the star quality that trainers look for. But the usual tricks were, of course, needed, such as wires to move his lips when the horse "spoke." Nevertheless, Mr. Ed did have a pleasant personality, which made life easier for Alan Young and for the horse's trainer, Les Hilton.

The same could not be said for television's most famous chimpanzee, J. Fred Muggs. You need a long memory to recall Muggs, since he flourished in what we now regard as the earlier days of television—those days when Dave Garroway was host of the "Today" show, which means five or six hosts ago.

In those days, the 1950s and 1960s, J. Fred Muggs was all over television. There are pictures of him with Garroway and with such stars as Bob Hope, Jayne Mansfield, and Peter Lawford. The chimp even was listed as president of J. Fred Muggs Enterprises, an industry built on his acting skills. (The brains of the outfit was Carmine Menella, who was the chimpanzee's trainer.)

The first point to note is that unlike Cheetah, the other famous chimpanzee of the screen, Muggs was noted not for his acting ability but for pure personality. Cheetah achieved success by being involved in

J. Fred Muggs, the television star, in a scholarly mood.

plots; he would laugh when Tarzan did something funny, hide his face when Boy did something embarrassing, and carry messages or untie a rope or do whatever else was necessary to make sure the good guys won in the end. By contrast, J. Fred Muggs made his mark simply by being part of the gang on television talk shows. It was a road to success that has been followed by many human actors since then—actors who have discovered that in the new TV era, acting skill is less important than the ability to swap chitchat with the host on a talk show.

A more interesting point about J. Fred Muggs is that he did not seem to be the most pleasant character if the testimony of the humans who worked with him was to be trusted. One must tread carefully in discussing these reports, because J. Fred Muggs has the distinction of being one of the few animals to sue a television network for the equivalent of libel. In 1957, Menella charged NBC and Garroway with an alleged conspiracy to injure the chimpanzee's reputation by making statements on the air about Muggs biting people. The case dragged on for six years, and NBC finally settled out of court for what was described as a modest sum. (Menella's explanation for the alleged bites was that Fred would clamp his teeth affectionately on someone's hand and that the object of his affections would hurt himself by jerking the hand away.)

The point about J. Fred Muggs was that toward the end of his career he was not one of the young, pleasant chimpanzees who are easy to handle. As has been noted, chimps become more difficult as they grow older. There were reports that J. Fred Muggs had to be disciplined with a battery-powered electric shocker to keep him in line—a charge that Menella denied. There were countercharges that Frank Blair, the news broadcaster on the "Today" show, once stole a tricycle on which J. Fred Muggs performed, and that staff members maliciously left a door open so that a draft could enter when Fred had a cold. (For those who do not rise early, it should be noted that the "Today" show is a mixture of interviews, news reports, and features that is shown as the sun rises.) Despite all the acrimony, the image created by Fred's television appearances produced a brisk demand for his services on the stage and at such events as the opening of shopping centers—enough to bring his income up to $50,000 a year.

The other great animal star who owed his success to television alone was Morris the cat. Like many other animal stars, Morris had a humble beginning. His trainer, Bob Martwick, picked him out of an animal shelter in Chicago in 1966. Martwick, who saw possibilities in Morris' insouciant manner and goldish-orange fur, later sold the cat to the Nine Lives Cat Food Company, which made him the star of its commercials. In a ten-year period, Morris made forty commercials and became a nationally known personality.

Morris had the usual benefits of stardom. He traveled in limousines, stayed in luxury hotels, and had the best of care. His owners had to fly him around the

Morris the cat, caught in a reflective moment when he was not eating his sponsor's cat food.

country in an unmarked cage, to keep him from being mobbed by his fans. Morris even had the ultimate in celebrity attention, his own public relations representatives to handle press requests. While Morris did make one film appearance, with Burt Reynolds in *Shamus* (1973), his appeal was essentially the result of the commercials in which he was portrayed as a sophisticated, aloof gourmet who would unbend only when he was offered some Nine Lives Cat Food.

Morris was unquestionably a celebrity. When he died in 1978, at what was believed to be an advanced age, the major wire services and television stations all carried obituaries, and a few newspapers ran affectionate feature stories. Nine Lives even pulled all its Morris commercials off the air for a few days in respect—although there was another Morris waiting in the wings to carry on when the mourning period was over.

Morris thus was one of the few animals to break through the main barrier to fame on television. That barrier is the fleeting nature of television success, which is quite different from the Hollywood style. Any movie, however mediocre, never quite fades away completely. There is always a revival theater or a television channel that will bring a film back for one more showing. It is even possible to see such film nonclassics as *Bedtime for Bonzo* (1951), in which Ronald Reagan played opposite Bonzo the chimp. It was Reagan's last film appearance—and one which, in his new capacity as distinguished politician, he would just as soon forget. But with a few exceptions, television series have a way of vanishing without a trace.

Despite all his past fame, J. Fred Muggs today is known chiefly to aging television trivia fans. And does anyone remember the basset hound Cleo, who was a star of a 1950s television series called "The People's Choice"? The show's human star was Jackie Cooper, who played a small-town mayor. Cleo delivered a running commentary on the plot, somewhat in the style of Mr. Ed. (The voice was supplied by an actress and the lip movements by wires.) Hardly anyone recalls Cleo these days, even though the show ran for years.

More recently, as the monetary stakes in television have grown and the pace has become more frantic, series have begun to disappear even more rapidly and thoroughly. It is quite common for a series to be killed after only a few weeks if the ratings are not right. That makes it tougher for animals as well as human actors. A viewer who blinked might have missed the 1978 series "Sam," in which Sam was a canine cop, a dog who solved cases that left his human police partner helpless. The gimmick didn't work and Sam went back to the kennel. Television, however, obviously will keep trying similar gimmicks, such as having a chimp named Bear in the series titled "BJ and the Bear." (BJ was a trucker who would accept any cargo at all.)

Obviously, television has a style all its own—a style that has a strong effect on the kind of imaginary animals who achieve TV stardom. In the movies, most imaginary animals tend to be huge, like King Kong and Godzilla. On television, most imaginary animals are small, so that they can fit the TV screen. In fact, almost all of the most successful imaginary animals on television have been puppets. In the early days, there was Ollie, the dragon on the long-running "Kukla, Fran, and Ollie." Kukla was a round-headed, amusing little puppet man, and Fran was Fran Allison, a charming woman who gave the puppets advice, comfort, and love. The puppet master was Burr Tillstrom, who made a brief appearance at the end of every show.

Then there was "Time for Beany," a puppet show that flourished in the early 1950s. "Time for Beany" was created by Bob Clampett, the cartoonist who was also responsible for Bugs Bunny, and it featured Cecil the Sea Sick Sea Serpent, the Fat Bat, Ping Pong the Giant Ape, Tearalong the dotted lion, and Smarty Pants the frog, among other imaginary beings. "Time for Beany" was enormously successful for more than a decade. The stars who appeared on the show included Jerry Lewis, Liberace, Mel Torme, and Spike Jones. It is said that in the 1950s, when Louis B. Mayer, the head of MGM, banned all television sets from the studio because he thought TV was a threat to the movie business.

The "Time for Beany" puppet characters were transformed into animated cartoons in 1962. The cartoons not only were successful in movie theaters but

Big Bird, an animal star of "Sesame Street," with the rest of the cast. (Children's Television Workshop)

also had a long run on television. But once again, when that run ended, "Time for Beany" began to fade from public attention. The adults who were children when "Time for Beany" was on the air still recall it, but to youngsters today the show is nothing but a name out of the dim past.

The outlook is much more promising for the puppet characters who were created for the educational television show "Sesame Street." Big Bird (an eight-foot, five-hundred-pound canary), the Cooky Monster, Snuffle-upagus the elephant, and Oscar the Grouch have been on TV for more than a decade now, and there is no reason why they can't go on for another decade. "Sesame Street" was created by the Children's Television Workshop to help young children learn the basic skills of reading, writing, and arithmetic. The show has been a success beyond anyone's early expectations, proving not only that television could really be educational but also that shows for children on television could have wit and quality. The existence of "Sesame Street" did pull the level of children's programming on the television networks up a notch or two, although that level was still anything but elevated.

The standard network television show for children, made to be shown on Saturday mornings, consisted of made-for-TV cartoons wrapped around commercials for breakfast foods and toys. A host of animal characters have been created for television—Yogi Bear, Tennessee Tuxedo, Rocky the Flying Squirrel and his friend, Bullwinkle the Moose, Mighty Mouse, Wonder Dog, and many more. At their best, TV cartoon shows can be genuinely amusing. At their worst, they are truly chewing gum for the mind, something to watch with glazed eyes. The one point that is made by animators who learned their skills in the era when

Walt Disney had set new standards for cartoons is that animation today is nothing like it used to be. Television's hunger for new material and its low budgets make it impossible to spend the kind of time and money needed to produce high-quality animations.

But commercial television has shown that it has room for some marvelously imaginative puppet animals. "The Muppet Show," created by the puppeteer Jim Henson, has been one of the most popular shows on television, not only in the United States but in seventy-two other countries as well. Led by Kermit the Frog (constantly being chased by Miss Piggy, a character with romance in mind), the Muppets include Fozzie Bear, Dr. Julius Strangepork, Sam the Eagle and, as they say, a host of other characters.

The Muppets look like pure fun on television, but producing each show requires hours of precision work by Henson's staff in his English studio. The Muppets are close to life-sized puppets, and manipulating them so that all the gags work right takes a lot of work. (For those who are curious, Kermit is played by Jim Henson himself, while Fozzie is played by a Henson sidekick named Frank Oz—no relative of the wizard.) The Muppet shows have smoothly integrated appearances by most of the big names on television such as the likes of Pearl Bailey, Raquel Welch, Liberace, Helen Reddy, Cheryl Ladd, and Don Knotts.

And a reminder of what commercial television could do with cartoon animal characters has been provided continually by "The Wonderful World of Disney," a

Miss Piggy, a leading player in "The Muppets."

long-running series whose backbone is the material that the Disney studio produced for the movies. Perhaps wisely, the Disney organization never entered the scramble to produce low-budget cartoons for television consumption. Instead, it brought back the old, high-quality cartoons in carefully measured amounts and at carefully timed intervals, knowing that the material could be used over and over as child viewers graduated to more mature television fare and were replaced by fresh young TV audiences. For many years, the same material was shown on the "Mickey Mouse Club," a Monday-to-Friday half-hour show that also featured a band of human actors named the Mouseketeers. They all wore beanies with big mouse ears, which promptly sprouted on children's heads all over the country. The Mouseketeers went off the air after a while, fading into the realm of television trivia games, but the memory of the great Disney cartoons lives on.

With all due respect to television, it is hard to resist the conclusion that aside from a few bright spots—such as the Muppets, the band of puppets led by Kermit the Frog—its best efforts almost always are a cut below those of the movies. For example, the success of the film *Star Wars* led to an ABC series titled "Battlestar Galactica," which used the same special-effects team that had worked on the film hit. The "Battlestar Galactica" version of a futuristic animal was a mechanical dog called a Daggit, which was actually a chimpanzee named Evolution in a furry space suit.

The barroom full of strange creatures from other star systems was beyond the resources of television.

Unhappily, as the 1970s turned into the 1980s, it began to seem that the great days of animals on the screen—TV screen and movie screen alike—were over. Animal stars achieved their greatest popularity in the days of the movie's innocence, when audiences were willing to accept warm sentimentality and bright-eyed dreams as a realistic picture of the American scene. In the hard-eyed world of the 1980s, where sex and violence are everywhere, the old innocence seems to be a thing of the past, and the old animal stars seem to be quaintly outmoded. Audiences seem to be in the mood for more slashing fare—tales of a killer shark, or a killer swarm of bees, or dolphins who are turned into killers by military villains.

But the picture isn't all bleak. The success of Benji and of Gentle Ben indicates that some of the old innocence survives. As a concluding note, it is worth re-mentioning that the story of Elsa the lioness had a happy ending. And that story came from real life.

Index

EDWARD EDELSON spends most of his working hours as the science editor of the New York *Daily News*, but he still manages to find the time to watch plenty of movies. A graduate of New York University and a Sloan-Rockefeller Fellow in the Advanced Science Writing Program at Columbia University, Mr. Edelson now lives in Jamaica, New York, with his wife and three children. His previous books include *Great Monsters of the Movies, The Book of Prophecy, Visions of Tomorrow, Funny Men of the Movies, Great Movie Spectaculars, Tough Guys and Gals of the Movies,* and *Great Kids of the Movies.*